Easy Home Cooking™

Country Casseroles

Country Casseroles

p. 4

p. 52

p. 68

Breakfast & Brunch

Egg & Sausage Casserole

½ pound pork sausage
3 tablespoons margarine or butter, divided
2 tablespoons all-purpose flour
¼ teaspoon salt
¼ teaspoon black pepper
1¼ cups milk

2 cups frozen hash brown potatoes
4 eggs, hard boiled and thinly sliced
½ cup cornflake crumbs
¼ cup sliced green onions
Fresh dill and oregano sprigs and chives (optional)

PREHEAT oven to 350°F. Spray 2-quart oval casserole with nonstick cooking spray. Crumble sausage into large skillet; brown over medium-high heat until no longer pink, stirring to separate sausage. Drain sausage on paper towels. Discard fat and wipe skillet with paper towel.

MELT 2 tablespoons margarine in same skillet over medium heat. Stir in flour, salt and pepper until smooth. Gradually stir in milk; cook and stir until thickened. Add sausage, potatoes and eggs; stir to combine. Pour into prepared dish. Melt remaining 1 tablespoon margarine. Combine cornflake crumbs and melted margarine in small bowl; sprinkle evenly over sausage mixture.

BAKE, uncovered, 30 minutes or until hot and bubbly. Sprinkle with onions. Garnish, if desired. *Makes 6 servings*

Nutrients per Serving: *Calories: 371, Total Fat: 23 g, Protein: 14 g, Carbohydrate: 27 g, Cholesterol: 167 mg, Sodium: 600 mg, Dietary Fiber: 1 g Dietary Exchanges: Bread: 2, Meat: 1, Fat: 4*

Mexican Roll-Ups with Avocado Sauce

8 eggs
2 tablespoons milk
1 tablespoon margarine or butter
1½ cups (6 ounces) shredded Monterey Jack cheese
1 large tomato, seeded and chopped
¼ cup chopped fresh cilantro
8 (6-inch) corn or flour tortillas

1½ cups salsa
2 medium avocados, chopped
¼ cup reduced-calorie sour cream
2 tablespoons diced green chilies
1 tablespoon fresh lemon juice
1 teaspoon hot pepper sauce
¼ teaspoon salt

PREHEAT oven to 350°F. Spray 13×9-inch baking dish with nonstick cooking spray.

WHISK eggs and milk in medium bowl until blended. Melt margarine in large skillet over medium heat; add egg mixture to skillet. Cook and stir 5 minutes or until eggs are set, but still soft. Remove from heat. Stir in cheese, tomato and cilantro.

SPOON about ⅓ cup egg mixture evenly down center of each tortilla. Roll up tortillas and place seam side down in prepared dish. Pour salsa evenly over tortillas. Cover tightly with foil and bake 20 minutes or until heated through.

Meanwhile, **PROCESS** avocados, sour cream, chilies, lemon juice, hot pepper sauce and salt in food processor or blender until smooth. Serve roll-ups with avocado sauce. *Makes 8 servings*

Nutrients per Serving: Calories: 316, Total Fat: 22 g, Protein: 15 g, Carbohydrate: 16 g, Cholesterol: 234 mg, Sodium: 665 mg, Dietary Fiber: 7 g Dietary Exchanges: Bread: 1, Meat: 1½, Fat: 3½

To reduce fat, omit avocado sauce and serve with additional salsa and nonfat sour cream.

Breakfast Pizza

1 can (10 ounces)
    refrigerated biscuit
    dough
½ pound bacon slices
2 tablespoons margarine or
    butter
2 tablespoons all-purpose
    flour

¼ teaspoon salt
⅛ teaspoon black pepper
1½ cups milk
½ cup (2 ounces) shredded
    sharp Cheddar cheese
¼ cup sliced green onions
¼ cup chopped red bell
    pepper

PREHEAT oven to 350°F. Spray 13×9-inch baking dish with nonstick cooking spray.

SEPARATE biscuit dough and arrange side by side in rectangle on lightly floured surface without overlapping. Roll into 14×10-inch rectangle. Place in prepared dish; pat edges up sides of dish. Bake 15 minutes. Remove from oven and set aside.

Meanwhile, **PLACE** bacon in single layer in large skillet; cook over medium heat until crisp. Remove from skillet; drain on paper towels. Crumble and set aside.

MELT margarine in medium saucepan over medium heat. Stir in flour, salt and black pepper until smooth. Gradually stir in milk; cook and stir until thickened. Stir in cheese until melted. Spread sauce evenly over baked crust. Sprinkle bacon, green onions and bell pepper over sauce.

BAKE, uncovered, 20 minutes or until crust is golden brown.

Makes 6 servings

Nutrients per Serving: Calories: 280, Total Fat: 14 g, Protein: 10 g, Carbohydrate: 29 g, Cholesterol: 18 mg, Sodium: 793 mg, Dietary Fiber: 1 g Dietary Exchanges: Bread: 2, Meat: ½, Fat: 2½

Chili Cheese Puff

∙∙∙

¾ **cup all-purpose flour**
1½ **teaspoons baking powder**
9 **eggs**
4 **cups (16 ounces)**
   shredded Monterey
   Jack cheese
2 **cups (1 pint) 1% milkfat**
   cottage cheese

2 **cans (4 ounces each)**
   diced green chilies,
   drained
1½ **teaspoons sugar**
¼ **teaspoon salt**
⅛ **teaspoon hot pepper**
   sauce
1 **cup salsa**

PREHEAT oven to 350°F. Spray 13×9-inch baking dish with nonstick cooking spray.

COMBINE flour and baking powder in small bowl.

WHISK eggs in large bowl until blended; add Monterey Jack cheese, cottage cheese, chilies, sugar, salt and hot pepper sauce. Add flour mixture; stir just until combined. Pour into prepared dish.

BAKE, uncovered, 45 minutes or until egg mixture is set. Let stand 5 minutes before serving. Serve with salsa.   *Makes 8 servings*

Nutrients per Serving: Calories: 393, Total Fat: 23 g, Protein: 29 g, Carbohydrate: 14 g, Cholesterol: 292 mg, Sodium: 1060 mg, Dietary Fiber: 2 g Dietary Exchanges: Bread: 1, Meat: 4, Fat: 2

Substitute a jalapeño pepper for the diced green chilies. Seed and dice the jalapeño and add to egg mixture. Be careful when handling pepper because it can sting and irritate the skin. Wash hands after handling.

Menu

Chili Cheese Puff

Sausage Patties

Mango or Papaya Slices

Assorted Muffins

Orange Juice

Apple & Raisin Oven Pancake

1 large baking apple, cored
   and thinly sliced
⅓ cup golden raisins
2 tablespoons packed
   brown sugar
½ teaspoon ground
   cinnamon
4 eggs

⅔ cup milk
⅔ cup all-purpose flour
2 tablespoons margarine or
   butter, melted
Powdered sugar
   (optional)
Raspberries and fresh
   herb (optional)

PREHEAT oven to 350°F. Spray 9-inch pie plate with nonstick cooking spray.

COMBINE apple, raisins, brown sugar and cinnamon in medium bowl. Transfer to prepared pie plate.

BAKE, uncovered, 10 to 15 minutes or until apple begins to soften. Remove from oven. *Increase oven temperature to 450°F.*

Meanwhile, **WHISK** eggs, milk, flour and margarine in medium bowl until blended. Pour batter over apple mixture.

BAKE 15 minutes or until pancake is golden brown. Sprinkle with powdered sugar, if desired. Garnish with raspberries and herb, if desired.
Makes 6 servings

Nutrients per Serving: Calories: 207, Total Fat: 8 g, Protein: 7 g, Carbohydrate: 28 g, Cholesterol: 144 mg, Sodium: 103 mg, Dietary Fiber: 1 g
Dietary Exchanges: Fruit: 1, Bread: 1, Meat: ½, Fat: ½

Cook's Nook

Apple varieties best for baking are Cortland, Northern Spy, Rome Beauty, Winesap and York Imperial.

French Toast Strata

....

4 ounces day-old French or
  Italian bread, cut into
  ¾-inch cubes (4 cups)
⅓ cup golden raisins
1 package (3 ounces)
  cream cheese, cut into
  ¼-inch cubes
3 eggs
1½ cups milk

½ cup maple-flavored
  pancake syrup
1 teaspoon vanilla
2 tablespoons sugar
1 teaspoon ground
  cinnamon
Additional maple-flavored
  pancake syrup
  (optional)

SPRAY 11×7-inch baking dish with nonstick cooking spray. Place bread cubes in even layer in prepared dish; sprinkle raisins and cream cheese evenly over bread.

BEAT eggs in medium bowl with electric mixer at medium speed until blended. Add milk, ½ cup pancake syrup and vanilla; mix well. Pour egg mixture evenly over bread mixture. Cover; refrigerate at least 4 hours or overnight.

PREHEAT oven to 350°F. Combine sugar and cinnamon in small bowl; sprinkle evenly over bread mixture.

BAKE, uncovered, 40 to 45 minutes or until puffy, golden brown and knife inserted in center comes out clean. Cut into squares and serve with additional pancake syrup, if desired.   *Makes 6 servings*

Nutrients per Serving: *Calories: 287, Total Fat: 9 g, Protein: 8 g, Carbohydrate: 44 g, Cholesterol: 127 mg, Sodium: 237 mg, Dietary Fiber: trace*
Dietary Exchanges: Fruit: 1, Bread: 2, Meat: ½, Fat: 1

Beef & Pork

Chili Spaghetti Casserole

8 ounces uncooked
   spaghetti
1 pound lean ground beef
1 medium onion, chopped
¼ teaspoon salt
⅛ teaspoon black pepper
1 can (15 ounces)
   vegetarian chili with
   beans
1 can (14½ ounces) Italian-
   style stewed tomatoes,
   undrained

1½ cups (6 ounces) shredded
   sharp Cheddar cheese,
   divided
½ cup reduced-fat sour
   cream
1½ teaspoons chili powder
¼ teaspoon garlic powder

PREHEAT oven to 350°F. Spray 13×9-inch baking dish with nonstick cooking spray.

COOK pasta according to package directions until al dente. Drain and place in prepared dish.

Meanwhile, **PLACE** beef and onion in large skillet; sprinkle with salt and pepper. Brown beef over medium-high heat until beef is no longer pink, stirring to separate beef. Drain fat. Stir in chili, tomatoes with juice, 1 cup cheese, sour cream, chili powder and garlic powder.

ADD chili mixture to pasta; stir until pasta is well coated. Sprinkle with remaining ½ cup cheese.

COVER tightly with foil and bake 30 minutes or until hot and bubbly. Let stand 5 minutes before serving.   *Makes 8 servings*

Nutrients per Serving: Calories: 347, Total Fat: 13 g, Protein: 23 g, Carbohydrate: 32 g, Cholesterol: 51 mg, Sodium: 414 mg, Dietary Fiber: 4 g Dietary Exchanges: Vegetable: 1, Bread: 1½, Meat: 2½, Fat: 1½

Ham, Barley and Almond Bake

½ cup slivered almonds
1 tablespoon margarine or
  butter
1 cup uncooked barley
1 cup chopped carrots
1 bunch green onions,
  sliced
2 ribs celery, sliced
3 cloves garlic, minced
1 pound lean smoked ham,
  cubed
2 teaspoons dried basil
  leaves

1 teaspoon dried oregano
  leaves
¼ teaspoon black pepper
2 cans (14 ounces each)
  reduced-sodium beef
  broth
½ pound fresh green beans,
  cut into 1-inch pieces
  Fresh basil sprig and
  carrot ribbons
  (optional)

PREHEAT oven to 350°F. Spray 13×9-inch baking dish with nonstick cooking spray.

SPREAD almonds in single layer on baking sheet. Bake 5 minutes or until golden brown, stirring frequently.

MELT margarine in large skillet over medium-high heat. Add barley, chopped carrots, onions, celery and garlic; cook and stir 2 minutes or until onions are tender. Remove from heat. Stir in ham, almonds, dried basil, oregano and pepper. Pour into prepared dish.

POUR broth into medium saucepan; bring to a boil over high heat. Pour over barley mixture.

COVER tightly with foil and bake 20 minutes. Remove from oven; stir in green beans. Bake, covered, 30 minutes or until barley is tender. Garnish with fresh basil and carrot ribbons, if desired.

Makes 8 servings

Nutrients per Serving: Calories: 232, Total Fat: 7 g, Protein: 19 g,
Carbohydrate: 27 g, Cholesterol: 32 mg, Sodium: 666 mg, Dietary Fiber: 5 g
Dietary Exchanges: Vegetable: 1, Bread: 1½, Meat: 2

Hearty Biscuit-Topped Steak Pie

1½ pounds top round steak, cooked and cut into 1-inch cubes

1 package (9 ounces) frozen baby carrots

1 package (9 ounces) frozen peas and pearl onions

1 large baking potato, cooked, peeled and cut into ½-inch pieces

1 jar (18 ounces) home-style brown gravy

½ teaspoon dried thyme leaves

½ teaspoon black pepper

1 can (12 ounces) refrigerated flaky buttermilk biscuits

PREHEAT oven to 375°F. Spray 11×7-inch baking dish with nonstick cooking spray.

COMBINE steak, frozen vegetables and potato in prepared dish. Stir in gravy, thyme and pepper.

BAKE, uncovered, 40 minutes. Remove from oven. *Increase oven temperature to 400°F.* Top with biscuits and bake 8 to 10 minutes or until biscuits are golden brown.   *Makes 6 servings*

Nutrients per Serving: Calories: 413, Total Fat: 14 g, Protein: 34 g, Carbohydrate: 37 g, Cholesterol: 58 mg, Sodium: 1029 mg, Dietary Fiber: 2 g Dietary Exchanges: Vegetable: 1, Bread: 2, Meat: 3½, Fat: 1

This casserole can be prepared with leftovers of almost any kind. Other steaks, roast beef, stew meat, pork, lamb or chicken can be substituted for round steak; adjust gravy flavor to complement meat. Red potatoes can be used in place of baking potato. Choose your favorite vegetable combination as a substitute for the peas, onions and carrots.

Family-Style Hot Dogs with Red Beans and Rice

1 tablespoon vegetable oil
1 medium onion, chopped
½ medium green bell
    pepper, chopped
2 cloves garlic, minced
1 can (14 ounces) red
    kidney beans, drained
    and rinsed
1 can (14 ounces) Great
    Northern beans,
    drained and rinsed

½ pound beef hot dogs, cut
    into ¼-inch-thick slices
1 cup uncooked instant
    brown rice
1 cup vegetable broth
¼ cup ketchup
¼ cup packed brown sugar
3 tablespoons dark
    molasses
1 tablespoon Dijon mustard
    Zucchini ribbons (optional)

PREHEAT oven to 350°F. Spray 13×9-inch baking dish with nonstick cooking spray.

HEAT oil in Dutch oven over medium-high heat until hot. Add onion, pepper and garlic; cook and stir 2 minutes or until onion is tender.

ADD beans, hot dogs, rice, broth, ketchup, sugar, molasses and mustard to vegetables; stir to combine. Pour into prepared dish.

COVER tightly with foil and bake 30 minutes or until rice is tender. Garnish with zucchini, if desired. *Makes 6 servings*

Nutrients per Serving: Calories: 475, Total Fat: 15 g, Protein: 18 g, Carbohydrate: 72 g, Cholesterol: 23 mg, Sodium: 714 mg, Dietary Fiber: 7 g Dietary Exchanges: Vegetable: 1, Bread: 3, Meat: 1, Fat: 4

Smoked sausage can be substituted for hot dogs. Cut sausage into ¼-inch-thick slices and add with beans.

Beefy Nacho Crescent Bake

....

1 pound lean ground beef
½ cup chopped onion
¼ teaspoon salt
⅛ teaspoon black pepper
1 tablespoon chili powder
1 teaspoon ground cumin
1 teaspoon dried oregano
   leaves
1 can (11 ounces)
   condensed nacho
   cheese soup, undiluted

1 cup milk
1 can (8 ounces)
   refrigerated crescent
   roll dough
¼ cup (1 ounce) shredded
   Cheddar cheese
Chopped fresh cilantro
   (optional)
Salsa (optional)

PREHEAT oven to 375°F. Spray 13×9-inch baking dish with nonstick cooking spray.

PLACE beef and onion in large skillet; sprinkle with salt and pepper. Brown beef over medium-high heat until no longer pink, stirring to separate beef. Drain fat. Stir in chili powder, cumin and oregano. Cook and stir 2 minutes; remove from heat.

COMBINE soup and milk in medium bowl, stirring until smooth. Pour soup mixture into prepared dish, spreading evenly.

SEPARATE crescent dough into 4 rectangles; press perforations together firmly. Roll out each rectangle to 8×4 inches. Cut each rectangle in half crosswise to form 8 (4-inch) squares.

SPOON about ¼ cup beef mixture in center of each square. Lift 4 corners of dough up over filling to meet in center; pinch and twist firmly to seal. Place squares in dish.

BAKE, uncovered, 20 to 25 minutes or until crusts are golden brown. Sprinkle cheese over squares. Bake 5 minutes or until cheese melts. To serve, spoon soup mixture over each serving; sprinkle with cilantro, if desired. Serve with salsa, if desired.

Makes 4 servings

Nutrients per Serving: Calories: 564, Total Fat: 35 g, Protein: 31 g, Carbohydrate: 35 g, Cholesterol: 93 mg, Sodium: 1260 mg, Dietary Fiber: 3 g Dietary Exchanges: Bread: 2, Meat: 3, Fat: 5½

Reuben Noodle Bake

8 ounces uncooked egg
　　noodles
5 ounces thinly sliced
　　corned beef
1 can (14½ ounces)
　　sauerkraut with
　　caraway seeds, drained
2 cups (8 ounces) shredded
　　Swiss cheese
½ cup Thousand Island
　　dressing

½ cup milk
1 tablespoon prepared
　　mustard
2 slices pumpernickel
　　bread
1 tablespoon margarine or
　　butter, melted
Red onion slices
　　(optional)

PREHEAT oven to 350°F. Spray 13×9-inch baking dish with nonstick cooking spray.

COOK noodles according to package directions until al dente. Drain.

Meanwhile, **CUT** corned beef into bite-size pieces. Combine noodles, corned beef, sauerkraut and cheese in large bowl. Pour into prepared dish.

COMBINE dressing, milk and mustard in small bowl. Spoon dressing mixture evenly over noodle mixture.

TEAR bread into large pieces. Process in food processor or blender until crumbs are formed. Combine bread crumbs and margarine in small bowl; sprinkle evenly over casserole.

BAKE, uncovered, 25 to 30 minutes or until heated through. Garnish with red onion, if desired. *Makes 6 servings*

Serving Suggestion: Serve with a mixed green salad.

Nutrients per Serving: Calories: 456, Total Fat: 22 g, Protein: 23 g, Carbohydrate: 41 g, Cholesterol: 102 mg, Sodium: 1331 mg, Dietary Fiber: 1 g Dietary Exchanges: Vegetable: 1, Bread: 2½, Meat: 2, Fat: 3

Spicy Manicotti

3 cups ricotta cheese
1 cup grated Parmesan cheese, divided
2 eggs, lightly beaten
2½ tablespoons chopped fresh parsley
1 teaspoon dried Italian seasoning
½ teaspoon garlic powder
½ teaspoon salt
½ teaspoon black pepper

1 pound spicy Italian sausage, casing removed
1 can (28 ounces) crushed tomatoes in purée, undrained
1 jar (26 ounces) marinara or spaghetti sauce
8 ounces uncooked manicotti noodles

PREHEAT oven to 375°F. Spray 13×9-inch baking dish with nonstick cooking spray.

COMBINE ricotta cheese, ¾ cup Parmesan cheese, eggs, parsley, Italian seasoning, garlic powder, salt and pepper in medium bowl; set aside.

CRUMBLE sausage into large skillet; brown over medium-high heat until no longer pink, stirring to separate sausage. Drain sausage on paper towels; drain fat from skillet.

ADD tomatoes with juice and marinara sauce to same skillet; bring to a boil over high heat. Reduce heat to low; simmer, uncovered, 10 minutes. Pour about one third of sauce into prepared dish.

STUFF each uncooked noodle with about ½ cup cheese mixture. Place in dish. Top noodles with sausage; pour remaining sauce over noodles.

COVER tightly with foil and bake 50 minutes to 1 hour or until noodles are tender. Let stand 5 minutes before serving. Serve with remaining ¼ cup Parmesan cheese.   *Makes 8 servings*

Nutrients per Serving: Calories: 610, Total Fat: 38 g, Protein: 30 g, Carbohydrate: 38 g, Cholesterol: 154 mg, Sodium: 1660 mg, Dietary Fiber: 4 g Dietary Exchanges: Vegetable: 2, Bread: 2, Meat: 3, Fat: 5½

Menu

·············

Spicy Manicotti

Tossed Salad with
Vinaigrette Dressing

Garlic Bread

Italian Ice

Coffee

Pork Chops and Apple Stuffing

6 (¾-inch-thick) boneless pork loin chops (about 1½ pounds)
¼ teaspoon salt
⅛ teaspoon black pepper
1 tablespoon vegetable oil
1 small onion, chopped
2 ribs celery, chopped
2 Granny Smith apples, peeled, cored and coarsely chopped (about 2 cups)

1 can (14½ ounces) reduced-sodium chicken broth
1 can (10¾ ounces) condensed cream of celery soup, undiluted
¼ cup dry white wine
6 cups herb-seasoned stuffing cubes

PREHEAT oven to 375°F. Spray 13×9-inch baking dish with nonstick cooking spray.

SPRINKLE both sides of pork chops with salt and pepper. Heat oil in large deep skillet over medium-high heat until hot. Add pork chops and cook until browned on both sides, turning once. Remove from skillet; set aside.

ADD onion and celery to same skillet. Cook and stir 3 minutes or until onion is tender. Add apples; cook and stir 1 minute. Add broth, soup and wine; stir until smooth. Bring to a simmer; remove from heat. Stir in stuffing cubes until evenly moistened.

POUR stuffing mixture into prepared dish, spreading evenly. Place pork chops on top of stuffing; pour any accumulated juices over pork chops.

COVER tightly with foil and bake 30 to 40 minutes or until pork chops are juicy and barely pink in centers.   *Makes 6 servings*

Serving Suggestion: Serve with a mixed green salad.

Nutrients per Serving: Calories: 373, Total Fat: 15 g, Protein: 21 g, Carbohydrate: 38 g, Cholesterol: 59 mg, Sodium: 935 mg, Dietary Fiber: 2 g Dietary Exchanges: Vegetable: 1, Fruit: 1, Bread: 1, Meat: 2½, Fat: 2

Beef Stroganoff Casserole

1 pound lean ground beef
¼ teaspoon salt
⅛ teaspoon black pepper
1 teaspoon vegetable oil
8 ounces sliced
    mushrooms
1 large onion, chopped
3 cloves garlic, minced
¼ cup dry white wine
1 can (10¾ ounces)
    condensed cream of
    mushroom soup,
    undiluted

½ cup sour cream
1 tablespoon Dijon mustard
4 cups cooked egg noodles
    Chopped fresh parsley
    (optional)
    Radish slices and fresh
    Italian parsley sprigs
    (optional)

PREHEAT oven to 350°F. Spray 13×9-inch baking dish with nonstick cooking spray.

PLACE beef in large skillet; sprinkle with salt and pepper. Brown beef over medium-high heat until no longer pink, stirring to separate beef. Drain fat from skillet; set aside beef.

HEAT oil in same skillet over medium-high heat until hot. Add mushrooms, onion and garlic; cook and stir 2 minutes or until onion is tender. Add wine. Reduce heat to medium-low and simmer 3 minutes. Remove from heat; stir in soup, sour cream and mustard until well combined. Return beef to skillet.

PLACE noodles in prepared dish. Pour beef mixture over noodles; stir until noodles are well coated.

BAKE, uncovered, 30 minutes or until heated through. Sprinkle with chopped parsley, if desired. Garnish with radish and parsley sprigs, if desired.   *Makes 6 servings*

Nutrients per Serving: Calories: 419, Total Fat: 20 g, Protein: 21 g, Carbohydrate: 36 g, Cholesterol: 91 mg, Sodium: 596 mg, Dietary Fiber: 3 g Dietary Exchanges: Vegetable: 1, Bread: 2, Meat: 2, Fat: 3

Chicken & Turkey

Turkey & Green Bean Casserole

¼ cup slivered almonds
1 package (7 ounces) herb-seasoned stuffing cubes
¾ cup reduced-sodium chicken broth
1 can (10¾ ounces) condensed cream of mushroom soup, undiluted
¼ cup milk or half-and-half

¼ teaspoon black pepper
1 package (10 ounces) frozen French-style green beans, thawed and drained
2 cups diced cooked turkey or chicken (about ¾ pound)
Red bell pepper slices and fresh Italian parsley (optional)

PREHEAT oven to 350°F. Spray 11×7-inch baking dish with nonstick cooking spray. Spread almonds in single layer on baking sheet. Bake 5 minutes or until golden brown, stirring frequently. Set aside.

ADD stuffing to prepared dish; drizzle with broth. Stir to coat stuffing with broth. Combine soup, milk and black pepper in large bowl; stir in green beans and turkey. Spoon over stuffing; top with almonds.

BAKE, uncovered, 30 to 35 minutes or until heated through. Garnish with bell pepper and Italian parsley, if desired.   *Makes 4 servings*

Tip: Buying sliced turkey from the deli counter at your supermarket is a great way to save time when preparing a casserole. Just dice the turkey and add it to the casserole.

Nutrients per Serving: Calories: 403, Total Fat: 12 g, Protein: 22 g, Carbohydrate: 53 g, Cholesterol: 45 mg, Sodium: 1988 mg, Dietary Fiber: 2 g Dietary Exchanges: Vegetable: 1, Bread: 3, Meat: 1½, Fat: 2

Coq au Vin

½ cup all-purpose flour
1¼ teaspoons salt
¾ teaspoon black pepper
3½ pounds chicken pieces
2 tablespoons margarine or butter
8 ounces mushrooms, cut in half if large
4 cloves garlic, minced
¾ cup chicken broth

¾ cup dry red wine
2 teaspoons dried thyme leaves
1½ pounds red potatoes, quartered
2 cups frozen pearl onions (about 8 ounces)
Chopped fresh parsley (optional)

PREHEAT oven to 350°F.

COMBINE flour, salt and pepper in large resealable plastic food storage bag. Add chicken, two pieces at a time, and seal bag. Shake to coat chicken; remove chicken and set aside. Repeat with remaining pieces. Reserve remaining flour mixture.

MELT margarine in ovenproof Dutch oven over medium-high heat. Arrange chicken in single layer in Dutch oven and cook 3 minutes per side or until browned. Transfer to plate; set aside. Repeat with remaining pieces.

ADD mushrooms and garlic to Dutch oven; cook and stir 2 minutes. Sprinkle reserved flour mixture over mushroom mixture; cook and stir 1 minute. Add broth, wine and thyme; bring to a boil over high heat, stirring to scrape browned bits from bottom of Dutch oven. Add potatoes and onions; return to a boil. Remove from heat and place chicken in Dutch oven, partially covering chicken with broth mixture.

BAKE, covered, about 45 minutes or until chicken is no longer pink in centers, juices run clear and sauce is slightly thickened. Transfer chicken and vegetables to shallow bowls. Spoon sauce over chicken and vegetables. Sprinkle with parsley, if desired.

Makes 4 to 6 servings

Serving Suggestion: Serve with assorted fresh baked rolls.

Nutrients per Serving: Calories: 960, Total Fat: 37 g, Protein: 70 g, Carbohydrate: 79 g, Cholesterol: 198 mg, Sodium: 1154 mg, Dietary Fiber: 1 g Dietary Exchanges: Vegetable: 1, Bread: 5, Meat: 8, Fat: 3

Chicken Tetrazzini

8 ounces uncooked vermicelli, broken in half

1 can (10¾ ounces) condensed cream of mushroom soup, undiluted

¼ cup half-and-half

3 tablespoons dry sherry

½ teaspoon salt

⅛ to ¼ teaspoon crushed red pepper flakes

2 cups diced cooked chicken (about ¾ pound)

1 cup frozen peas

½ cup grated Parmesan cheese

1 cup fresh coarse bread crumbs

2 tablespoons margarine or butter, melted

Chopped fresh basil (optional)

Lemon slices and lettuce leaves (optional)

PREHEAT oven to 375°F. Spray 13×9-inch baking dish with nonstick cooking spray.

COOK pasta according to package directions until al dente. Drain.

Meanwhile, **COMBINE** soup, half-and-half, sherry, salt and pepper flakes in large bowl. Stir in chicken, peas and cheese. Add pasta to chicken mixture; stir until pasta is coated. Pour into prepared dish.

COMBINE bread crumbs and margarine in small bowl. Sprinkle evenly over casserole.

BAKE, uncovered, 25 to 30 minutes or until heated through and crumbs are golden brown. Sprinkle with basil, if desired. Garnish with lemon and lettuce, if desired.   *Makes 4 servings*

Nutrients per Serving: Calories: 614, Total Fat: 20 g, Protein: 40 g, Carbohydrate: 62 g, Cholesterol: 82 mg, Sodium: 2442 mg, Dietary Fiber: 2 g Dietary Exchanges: Bread: 4, Meat: 4, Fat: 2½

Turkey Meatball & Olive Casserole

2 cups uncooked rotini
    pasta
½ pound ground turkey
¼ cup dry bread crumbs
1 egg, slightly beaten
2 teaspoons dried minced
    onion
2 teaspoons white wine
    Worcestershire sauce
½ teaspoon dried Italian
    seasoning
½ teaspoon salt
⅛ teaspoon black pepper

1 tablespoon vegetable oil
1 can (10¾ ounces)
    condensed cream of
    celery soup, undiluted
½ cup low-fat plain yogurt
¾ cup pimiento-stuffed
    green olives, sliced
3 tablespoons Italian-style
    bread crumbs
1 tablespoon margarine or
    butter, melted
Paprika (optional)
Fresh herbs (optional)

PREHEAT oven to 350°F. Spray 2-quart round casserole with nonstick cooking spray.

COOK pasta according to package directions until al dente. Drain and set aside.

Meanwhile, **COMBINE** turkey, ¼ cup bread crumbs, egg, onion, Worcestershire, Italian seasoning, salt and pepper in medium bowl. Shape mixture into 1-inch meatballs.

HEAT oil in medium skillet over high heat until hot. Add meatballs in single layer; cook until lightly browned on all sides and still pink in centers, turning frequently. *Do not overcook.* Remove from skillet; drain on paper towels.

MIX soup and yogurt in large bowl. Add pasta, meatballs and olives; stir gently to combine. Transfer to prepared dish.

COMBINE 3 tablespoons bread crumbs and margarine in small bowl; sprinkle evenly over casserole. Sprinkle lightly with paprika, if desired.

BAKE, covered, 30 minutes. Uncover and bake 12 minutes or until meatballs are no longer pink in centers and casserole is hot and bubbly. Garnish with herbs, if desired.   *Makes 6 to 8 servings*

Nutrients per Serving: Calories: 337, Total Fat: 14 g, Protein: 15 g, Carbohydrate: 38 g, Cholesterol: 56 mg, Sodium: 1205 mg, Dietary Fiber: 1 g Dietary Exchanges: Bread: 2½, Meat: 1, Fat: 2

Chicken Pot Pie

2 tablespoons margarine or butter
¾ pound boneless skinless chicken breasts, cut into 1-inch pieces
¾ teaspoon salt
8 ounces fresh green beans, cut into 1-inch pieces (about 2 cups)
½ cup chopped red bell pepper
½ cup thinly sliced celery

3 tablespoons all-purpose flour
½ cup chicken broth
½ cup half-and-half
1 teaspoon dried thyme leaves
½ teaspoon rubbed sage
1 cup frozen pearl onions
½ cup frozen corn
Pastry for single-crust 10-inch pie

PREHEAT oven to 425°F. Spray 10-inch deep-dish pie plate with nonstick cooking spray.

MELT margarine in large deep skillet over medium-high heat. Add chicken; cook and stir 3 minutes or until no longer pink in centers. Sprinkle with salt. Add green beans, pepper and celery; cook and stir 3 minutes.

SPRINKLE flour evenly over chicken and vegetables; cook and stir 1 minute. Stir in broth, half-and-half, thyme and sage; bring to a boil over high heat. Reduce heat to low and simmer 3 minutes or until sauce is thickened. Stir in onions and corn. Return to a simmer; cook and stir 1 minute.

TRANSFER mixture to prepared pie plate. Place pie pastry over chicken mixture; turn pastry edge under and flute to seal. Cut 4 slits in pie pastry to allow steam to escape.

BAKE, uncovered, 20 minutes or until crust is light golden brown and chicken mixture is hot and bubbly. Let stand 5 minutes before serving. *Makes 6 servings*

Nutrients per Serving: Calories: 285, Total Fat: 15 g, Protein: 16 g, Carbohydrate: 22 g, Cholesterol: 43 mg, Sodium: 583 mg, Dietary Fiber: 1 g Dietary Exchanges: Vegetable: 1, Bread: 1, Meat: 1½, Fat: 2½

Indian-Spiced Chicken with Wild Rice

½ teaspoon salt
½ teaspoon ground cumin
½ teaspoon black pepper
¼ teaspoon ground
    cinnamon
¼ teaspoon ground
    turmeric
4 boneless skinless
    chicken breast halves
    (about 1 pound)
2 tablespoons olive oil
2 carrots, sliced

1 red bell pepper, chopped
1 rib celery, chopped
2 cloves garlic, minced
1 package (6 ounces) long
    grain and wild rice mix
2 cups reduced-sodium
    chicken broth
1 cup raisins
¼ cup sliced almonds
    Red bell pepper slices
    (optional)

COMBINE salt, cumin, black pepper, cinnamon and turmeric in small bowl. Rub spice mixture on both sides of chicken. Place chicken on plate; cover and refrigerate 30 minutes.

PREHEAT oven to 350°F. Spray 9-inch square baking dish with nonstick cooking spray.

HEAT oil in large skillet over medium-high heat until hot. Add chicken; cook 2 minutes per side or until browned. Transfer to clean plate; set aside.

PLACE carrots, chopped bell pepper, celery and garlic in same skillet. Cook and stir 2 minutes. Add rice; cook 5 minutes, stirring frequently. Add broth and seasoning packet from rice mix; bring to a boil over high heat. Remove from heat; stir in raisins. Pour into prepared dish; place chicken on rice mixture. Sprinkle with almonds.

COVER tightly with foil and bake 35 minutes or until chicken is no longer pink in centers, juices run clear and rice is tender. Garnish with bell pepper slices, if desired.   *Makes 4 servings*

Nutrients per Serving: Calories: 544, Total Fat: 17 g, Protein: 34 g, Carbohydrate: 67 g, Cholesterol: 69 mg, Sodium: 993 mg, Dietary Fiber: 4 g Dietary Exchanges: Vegetable: 2, Fruit: 2, Bread: 2, Meat: 3, Fat: 1½

Southern-Style Chicken and Greens

1 teaspoon salt
1 teaspoon paprika
½ teaspoon black pepper
3½ pounds chicken pieces
4 thick slices smoked
　　bacon (4 ounces), cut
　　crosswise into ¼-inch
　　pieces
1 cup uncooked rice
1 can (14½ ounces) stewed
　　tomatoes, undrained

1¼ cups chicken broth
2 cups packed coarsely
　　chopped fresh collard
　　or mustard greens or
　　kale (3 to 4 ounces)
Tomato wedges and
　　fresh Italian parsley
　　(optional)

PREHEAT oven to 350°F.

COMBINE salt, paprika and pepper in small bowl. Sprinkle meaty side of chicken pieces with salt mixture; set aside.

PLACE bacon in ovenproof Dutch oven; cook over medium heat until crisp. Drain on paper towels. Reserve bacon fat. Heat bacon fat over medium-high heat until hot. Arrange chicken in single layer in Dutch oven and cook 3 minutes per side or until browned. Transfer to clean plate; set aside. Repeat with remaining pieces. Reserve 1 tablespoon bacon fat in Dutch oven; discard remaining bacon fat.

ADD rice to Dutch oven; cook and stir 1 minute. Add tomatoes with juice, broth, collard greens and half of bacon; bring to a boil over high heat. Remove from heat; arrange chicken over rice mixture.

BAKE, covered, about 40 minutes or until chicken is no longer pink in centers, juices run clear and most of liquid is absorbed. Let stand 5 minutes before serving. Transfer to serving platter; sprinkle with remaining bacon. Garnish with tomato and Italian parsley, if desired.

Makes 4 to 6 servings

Nutrients per Serving: Calories: 906, Total Fat: 45 g, Protein: 74 g, Carbohydrate: 46 g, Cholesterol: 224 mg, Sodium: 1744 mg, Dietary Fiber: 1 g Dietary Exchanges: Vegetable: 2, Bread: 2½, Meat: 9, Fat: 4

Menu

Southern-Style Chicken and Greens

Corn Bread

Peach Cobbler with
Vanilla Ice Cream

Iced Tea and Lemonade

Chicken Marsala

6 ounces uncooked broad
  egg noodles
½ cup Italian-style dry
  bread crumbs
1 teaspoon dried basil
  leaves
1 egg
1 teaspoon water
4 boneless skinless
  chicken breast halves
3 tablespoons olive oil,
  divided
¾ cup chopped onion

8 ounces cremini or button
  mushrooms, sliced
3 cloves garlic, minced
3 tablespoons all-purpose
  flour
1 can (14½ ounces)
  chicken broth
½ cup dry marsala wine
¾ teaspoon salt
¼ teaspoon black pepper
  Chopped fresh parsley
  (optional)

PREHEAT oven to 375°F. Spray 11×7-inch baking dish with nonstick cooking spray. Cook noodles according to package directions until al dente. Drain and place in prepared dish.

Meanwhile, **COMBINE** bread crumbs and basil on shallow plate or pie plate. Beat egg with water on another shallow plate or pie plate. Dip chicken in egg mixture, letting excess drip off. Roll in crumb mixture, patting to coat. Heat 2 tablespoons oil in large skillet over medium-high heat until hot. Cook chicken 3 minutes per side or until browned. Transfer to clean plate; set aside.

HEAT remaining 1 tablespoon oil in same skillet over medium heat. Add onion; cook and stir 5 minutes. Add mushrooms and garlic; cook and stir 3 minutes. Sprinkle flour over onion mixture; cook and stir 1 minute. Add broth, wine, salt and pepper; bring to a boil over high heat. Cook and stir 5 minutes or until sauce thickens. Reserve ½ cup sauce. Pour remaining sauce over noodles; stir until noodles are well coated. Place chicken on top of noodles. Spoon reserved sauce over chicken.

BAKE, uncovered, 20 minutes or until chicken is no longer pink in centers. Sprinkle with parsley, if desired.   *Makes 4 servings*

Nutrients per Serving: Calories: 539, Total Fat: 19 g, Protein: 39 g, Carbohydrate: 49 g, Cholesterol: 175 mg, Sodium: 1224 mg, Dietary Fiber: 1 g Dietary Exchanges: Vegetable: 1, Bread: 3, Meat: 3, Fat: 3

Turkey and Biscuits

2 cans (10¾ ounces each)
  condensed cream of
  chicken soup, undiluted
¼ cup dry white wine
¼ teaspoon poultry
  seasoning
2 packages (8 ounces each)
  frozen cut asparagus,
  thawed

3 cups diced cooked turkey
  or chicken
Paprika (optional)
1 can (11 ounces)
  refrigerated flaky
  biscuits

PREHEAT oven to 350°F. Spray 13×9-inch baking dish with nonstick cooking spray.

COMBINE soup, wine and poultry seasoning in medium bowl.

ARRANGE asparagus in single layer in prepared dish. Place turkey evenly over asparagus. Spread soup mixture over turkey. Sprinkle lightly with paprika, if desired.

COVER tightly with foil and bake 20 minutes. Remove from oven. *Increase oven temperature to 425°F.* Top with biscuits and bake, uncovered, 8 to 10 minutes or until biscuits are golden brown.

Makes 6 servings

Nutrients per Serving: Calories: 369, Total Fat: 18 g, Protein: 18 g, Carbohydrate: 32 g, Cholesterol: 57 mg, Sodium: 1796 mg, Dietary Fiber: 2 g Dietary Exchanges: Vegetable: 1, Bread: 1½, Meat: 2, Fat: 3

Poultry seasoning is a powdered herb blend of sage, thyme, marjoram, savory, onion, black pepper and celery seed.

Artichoke-Olive Chicken Bake

1½ cups uncooked rotini pasta
1 tablespoon olive oil
1 medium onion, chopped
½ green bell pepper, chopped
2 cups shredded cooked chicken
1 can (14½ ounces) diced tomatoes with Italian-style herbs, undrained

1 can (14 ounces) artichoke hearts, drained and quartered
1 can (6 ounces) sliced black olives, drained
1 teaspoon dried Italian seasoning
2 cups (8 ounces) shredded mozzarella cheese
Fresh basil sprig (optional)

PREHEAT oven to 350°F. Spray 13×9-inch baking dish with nonstick cooking spray.

COOK pasta according to package directions until al dente. Drain and set aside.

Meanwhile, **HEAT** oil in large deep skillet over medium heat until hot. Add onion and pepper; cook and stir 1 minute. Add chicken, tomatoes with juice, pasta, artichokes, olives and Italian seasoning; mix until combined.

PLACE half of chicken mixture in prepared dish; sprinkle with half of cheese. Top with remaining chicken mixture and cheese.

BAKE, covered, 35 minutes or until hot and bubbly. Garnish with basil, if desired.

Makes 8 servings

Nutrients per Serving: Calories: 369, Total Fat: 18 g, Protein: 21 g, Carbohydrate: 34 g, Cholesterol: 43 mg, Sodium: 1497 mg, Dietary Fiber: 7 g Dietary Exchanges: Vegetable: 3, Bread: 1, Meat: 2, Fat: 2½

Serve with crusty Italian or French bread and a tossed salad.

Roasted Chicken and Vegetables over Wild Rice

....

3½ pounds chicken pieces
¾ cup olive oil vinaigrette
    dressing, divided
1 tablespoon margarine or
    butter, melted
1 package (6 ounces) long
    grain and wild rice mix
1 can (13¾ ounces)
    reduced-sodium
    chicken broth
1 small eggplant, cut into
    1-inch pieces
2 medium red potatoes, cut
    into 1-inch pieces

1 medium yellow squash,
    cut into 1-inch pieces
1 medium zucchini, cut into
    1-inch pieces
1 medium red onion, cut
    into wedges
1 package (4 ounces)
    crumbled feta cheese
    with basil
Chopped fresh cilantro
    (optional)
Fresh thyme sprig
    (optional)

REMOVE skin from chicken; discard. Combine chicken and ½ cup dressing in large resealable plastic food storage bag. Seal bag and turn to coat. Refrigerate 30 minutes or overnight.

PREHEAT oven to 375°F. Coat bottom of 13×9-inch baking dish with margarine.

ADD rice and seasoning packet to prepared dish; stir in broth. Combine eggplant, potatoes, squash, zucchini and onion in large bowl. Place on top of rice mixture.

REMOVE chicken from bag and place on top of vegetables; discard marinade. Pour remaining ¼ cup dressing over chicken.

BAKE, uncovered, 45 minutes. Remove from oven and sprinkle with cheese. Bake 5 to 10 minutes or until chicken is no longer pink in centers, juices run clear and cheese is melted. Sprinkle with cilantro, if desired. Garnish with thyme, if desired.   *Makes 4 to 6 servings*

Nutrients per Serving: Calories: 858, Total Fat: 42 g, Protein: 47 g, Carbohydrate: 70 g, Cholesterol: 125 mg, Sodium: 1092 mg, Dietary Fiber: 1 g Dietary Exchanges: Vegetable: 2, Bread: 4, Meat: 4½, Fat: 6

Fish & Shellfish

Flounder Fillets over Zesty Lemon Rice

¼ cup margarine or butter
3 tablespoons fresh lemon
  juice
2 teaspoons chicken
  bouillon granules
½ teaspoon black pepper
1 cup cooked rice
1 package (10 ounces)
  frozen chopped
  broccoli, thawed

1 cup (4 ounces) shredded
  sharp Cheddar cheese
1 pound flounder fillets
½ teaspoon paprika
  Lemon slices, lemon peel
  and fresh parsley
  (optional)

PREHEAT oven to 375°F. Spray 2-quart square casserole with nonstick cooking spray.

MELT margarine in small saucepan over medium heat. Add lemon juice, bouillon and pepper; cook and stir 2 minutes or until bouillon is dissolved.

COMBINE rice, broccoli, cheese and ¼ cup lemon sauce in medium bowl; spread on bottom of prepared dish. Place fillets on top of rice mixture. Pour remaining lemon sauce over fillets.

BAKE, uncovered, 20 minutes or until fish flakes easily when tested with fork. Sprinkle evenly with paprika. Garnish with lemon and parsley, if desired.   *Makes 6 servings*

Nutrients per Serving: Calories: 263, Total Fat: 12 g, Protein: 25 g, Carbohydrate: 12 g, Cholesterol: 61 mg, Sodium: 650 mg, Dietary Fiber: 1 g Dietary Exchanges: Vegetable: 1, Bread: ½, Meat: 3, Fat: 1

Tuna Noodle Casserole

7 ounces uncooked elbow macaroni

2 tablespoons margarine or butter

¾ cup chopped onion

½ cup thinly sliced celery

½ cup finely chopped red bell pepper

2 tablespoons all-purpose flour

1 teaspoon salt

⅛ teaspoon ground white pepper

1½ cups milk

1 can (6 ounces) albacore tuna in water, drained

½ cup grated Parmesan cheese, divided

Fresh dill sprigs (optional)

PREHEAT oven to 375°F. Spray 8-inch square baking dish with nonstick cooking spray.

COOK pasta according to package directions until al dente. Drain and set aside.

Meanwhile, **MELT** margarine in large deep skillet over medium heat. Add onion; cook and stir 3 minutes. Add celery and bell pepper; cook and stir 3 minutes. Sprinkle flour, salt and white pepper over vegetables; cook and stir 1 minute. Gradually stir in milk; cook and stir until thickened. Remove from heat.

ADD pasta, tuna and ¼ cup cheese to skillet; stir until pasta is well coated. Pour tuna mixture into prepared dish; sprinkle evenly with remaining ¼ cup cheese.

BAKE, uncovered, 20 to 25 minutes or until hot and bubbly. Garnish with dill, if desired. *Makes 4 servings*

Nutrients per Serving: Calories: 424, Total Fat: 12 g, Protein: 27 g, Carbohydrate: 50 g, Cholesterol: 29 mg, Sodium: 1038 mg, Dietary Fiber: 1 g Dietary Exchanges: Vegetable: 1, Bread: 3, Meat: 2, Fat: 1½

Cook's Nook

Serve with spinach salad and warm biscuits.

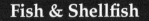

Jambalaya

1 teaspoon vegetable oil
½ pound smoked deli ham, cubed
½ pound smoked sausage, cut into ¼-inch-thick slices
1 large onion, chopped
1 large green bell pepper, chopped (about 1½ cups)
3 ribs celery, chopped (about 1 cup)
3 cloves garlic, minced
1 can (28 ounces) diced tomatoes, undrained

1 can (10½ ounces) chicken broth
1 cup uncooked rice
1 tablespoon Worcestershire sauce
1 teaspoon dried thyme leaves
1 teaspoon salt
½ teaspoon black pepper
¼ teaspoon ground red pepper
1 package (12 ounces) frozen ready-to-cook shrimp, thawed
Fresh chives (optional)

PREHEAT oven to 350°F. Spray 13×9-inch baking dish with nonstick cooking spray.

HEAT oil in large skillet over medium-high heat until hot. Add ham and sausage. Cook and stir 5 minutes or until sausage is lightly browned on both sides. Remove from skillet and place in prepared dish. Place onion, bell pepper, celery and garlic in same skillet; cook and stir 3 minutes. Add to sausage mixture.

COMBINE tomatoes with juice, broth, rice, Worcestershire, thyme, salt and black and red peppers in same skillet; bring to a boil over high heat. Reduce heat to low and simmer 3 minutes. Pour over sausage mixture and stir until combined.

COVER tightly with foil and bake 45 minutes or until rice is almost tender. Remove from oven; place shrimp on top of rice mixture. Bake, uncovered, 10 minutes or until shrimp are pink and opaque. Garnish with chives, if desired. *Makes 8 servings*

Nutrients per Serving: Calories: 285, Total Fat: 10 g, Protein: 20 g, Carbohydrate: 29 g, Cholesterol: 104 mg, Sodium: 1485 mg, Dietary Fiber: 1 g Dietary Exchanges: Vegetable: 2, Bread: 1, Meat: 2, Fat: 1

Pasta with Salmon and Dill

6 ounces uncooked mafalda
   pasta
1 tablespoon olive oil
2 ribs celery, sliced
1 small red onion, chopped
1 can (10¾ ounces)
   condensed cream of
   celery soup, undiluted
¼ cup reduced-fat
   mayonnaise
¼ cup dry white wine

3 tablespoons chopped
   fresh parsley
1 teaspoon dried dill weed
1 can (7½ ounces) pink
   salmon, drained
½ cup dry bread crumbs
1 tablespoon margarine or
   butter, melted
Fresh dill sprigs and red
   onion slices (optional)

PREHEAT oven to 350°F. Spray 1-quart square baking dish with nonstick cooking spray.

COOK pasta according to package directions until al dente. Drain and set aside.

Meanwhile, **HEAT** oil in medium skillet over medium-high heat until hot. Add celery and chopped onion; cook and stir 2 minutes or until vegetables are tender. Set aside.

COMBINE soup, mayonnaise, wine, parsley and dill weed in large bowl. Stir in pasta, vegetables and salmon until pasta is well coated. Pour salmon mixture into prepared dish.

COMBINE bread crumbs and margarine in small bowl; sprinkle evenly over casserole.

BAKE, uncovered, 25 minutes or until hot and bubbly. Garnish with fresh dill and red onion slices, if desired. *Makes 4 servings*

Nutrients per Serving: Calories: 468, Total Fat: 20 g, Protein: 18 g, Carbohydrate: 51 g, Cholesterol: 25 mg, Sodium: 988 mg, Dietary Fiber: 1 g Dietary Exchanges: Vegetable: 1, Bread: 3, Meat: 1, Fat: 4

Cook's Nook

Mafalda pasta is a broad, flat noodle with rippled edges that is similar to a small lasagna noodle.

Menu

Pasta with Salmon and Dill

Buttered Steamed Carrots

Focaccia Bread

White Wine

Tuna Pot Pie

1 tablespoon margarine or butter
1 small onion, chopped
1 can (10¾ ounces) condensed cream of potato soup, undiluted
¼ cup milk
½ teaspoon dried thyme leaves
¼ teaspoon salt
⅛ teaspoon black pepper
2 cans (6 ounces each) albacore tuna in water, drained

1 package (16 ounces) frozen vegetable medley (such as broccoli, green beans, pearl onions and red peppers), thawed
2 tablespoons chopped fresh parsley
1 can (8 ounces) refrigerated crescent roll dough

PREHEAT oven to 350°F. Spray 11×7-inch baking dish with nonstick cooking spray.

MELT margarine in large skillet over medium heat. Add onion; cook and stir 2 minutes or until onion is tender. Add soup, milk, thyme, salt and pepper; cook and stir 3 to 4 minutes or until thick and bubbly. Stir in tuna, vegetables and parsley. Pour mixture into prepared dish.

UNROLL crescent roll dough and separate into triangles. Place triangles over tuna mixture without overlapping dough.

BAKE, uncovered, 20 minutes or until triangles are golden brown. Let stand 5 minutes before serving. *Makes 6 servings*

Nutrients per Serving: Calories: 312, Total Fat: 13 g, Protein: 21 g, Carbohydrate: 31 g, Cholesterol: 27 mg, Sodium: 1076 mg, Dietary Fiber: 1 g Dietary Exchanges: Vegetable: 2, Bread: 1½, Meat: 2, Fat: 1

Create an exciting recipe by substituting a new vegetable medley for the one listed. Enjoy the results!

Creamy "Crab" Fettuccine

1 pound imitation crabmeat sticks

6 ounces uncooked fettuccine

3 tablespoons margarine or butter, divided

1 small onion, chopped

2 ribs celery, chopped

½ medium red bell pepper, chopped

2 cloves garlic, minced

1 cup reduced-fat sour cream

1 cup reduced-fat mayonnaise

1 cup (4 ounces) shredded sharp Cheddar cheese

2 tablespoons chopped fresh parsley

¼ teaspoon salt

⅛ teaspoon black pepper

½ cup cornflake crumbs
Fresh chives (optional)

PREHEAT oven to 350°F. Spray 2-quart square baking dish with nonstick cooking spray.

CUT crabmeat into bite-size pieces; set aside.

COOK pasta according to package directions until al dente. Drain and set aside.

Meanwhile, **MELT** 1 tablespoon margarine in large skillet over medium-high heat. Add onion, celery, bell pepper and garlic; cook and stir 2 minutes or until vegetables are tender. Set aside.

COMBINE sour cream, mayonnaise, cheese, parsley, salt and black pepper in large bowl. Add crabmeat, pasta and vegetable mixture, stirring gently to combine. Pour into prepared dish.

MELT remaining 2 tablespoons margarine. Combine cornflake crumbs and margarine in small bowl; sprinkle evenly over casserole.

BAKE, uncovered, 30 minutes or until hot and bubbly. Garnish with chives, if desired.   *Makes 6 servings*

Nutrients per Serving: Calories: 471, Total Fat: 24 g, Protein: 20 g, Carbohydrate: 42 g, Cholesterol: 51 mg, Sodium: 1140 mg, Dietary Fiber: 1 g
Dietary Exchanges: Vegetable: 1, Bread: 2½, Meat: 1½, Fat: 4

Vegetables & Sides

Mexican Tortilla Stack-Ups

1 tablespoon vegetable oil
½ cup chopped onion
1 can (15 ounces) black
    beans, drained and
    rinsed
1 can (14½ ounces)
    Mexican- or Italian-style
    diced tomatoes,
    undrained
1 cup frozen corn

1 envelope (1¼ ounces)
    taco seasoning mix
6 (6-inch) corn tortillas
2 cups (8 ounces) shredded
    Cheddar cheese with
    taco seasonings
1 cup water
    Sour cream (optional)
    Sliced black olives
    (optional)

PREHEAT oven to 350°F. Spray 13×9-inch baking dish with nonstick cooking spray.

HEAT oil in large skillet over medium-high heat until hot. Add onion; cook and stir 3 minutes or until tender. Add beans, tomatoes with juice, corn and taco seasoning mix. Bring to a boil over high heat. Reduce heat to low and simmer 5 minutes.

PLACE 2 tortillas side by side in prepared dish. Top each tortilla with about ½ cup bean mixture. Sprinkle evenly with one third of cheese. Repeat layers twice, creating 2 tortilla stacks each 3 tortillas high.

POUR water along sides of tortillas.

COVER tightly with foil and bake 30 to 35 minutes or until heated through. Cut into wedges to serve. Serve with sour cream and olives, if desired.

Makes 6 servings

Nutrients per Serving: Calories: 352, Total Fat: 16 g, Protein: 19 g, Carbohydrate: 38 g, Cholesterol: 40 mg, Sodium: 1031 mg, Dietary Fiber: 5 g Dietary Exchanges: Vegetable: 1, Bread: 2, Meat: 2, Fat: 1½

Easy Cheesy Lasagna

2 tablespoons olive oil
3 small zucchini, quartered lengthwise and thinly sliced crosswise
1 package (8 ounces) mushrooms, thinly sliced
1 medium onion, chopped
5 cloves garlic, minced
2 containers (15 ounces each) reduced-fat ricotta cheese
¼ cup grated Parmesan cheese
2 eggs

½ teaspoon dried Italian seasoning
¼ teaspoon garlic salt
⅛ teaspoon black pepper
1 can (28 ounces) crushed tomatoes in purée, undrained
1 jar (26 ounces) spaghetti sauce
1 package (16 ounces) lasagna noodles, uncooked
4 cups (16 ounces) shredded mozzarella cheese

PREHEAT oven to 375°F. Spray 13×9-inch baking dish or lasagna pan with nonstick cooking spray. Heat oil in large skillet over medium heat until hot. Add zucchini, mushrooms, onion and garlic; cook and stir 5 minutes.

COMBINE ricotta cheese, Parmesan cheese, eggs, Italian seasoning, garlic salt and pepper in medium bowl. Combine tomatoes and spaghetti sauce in another medium bowl.

SPREAD about ¾ cup tomato mixture in prepared dish. Place layer of uncooked noodles over tomato mixture, overlapping noodles. Spread half of vegetable mixture over noodles; top with half of ricotta cheese mixture. Sprinkle 1 cup mozzarella cheese over ricotta cheese mixture. Top with second layer of noodles. Spread about 1 cup tomato mixture over noodles. Top with remaining vegetable and ricotta cheese mixtures. Sprinkle with 1 cup mozzarella cheese. Top with third layer of noodles. Spread remaining tomato mixture over noodles. Sprinkle with remaining 2 cups mozzarella cheese.

COVER tightly with foil and bake 1 hour or until noodles in center are soft. Uncover; bake 5 minutes or until cheese is melted. Cover and let stand 15 minutes before serving. *Makes 10 to 12 servings*

Nutrients per Serving: Calories: 453, Total Fat: 19 g, Protein: 28 g, Carbohydrate: 45 g, Cholesterol: 96 mg, Sodium: 1072 mg, Dietary Fiber: 6 g
Dietary Exchanges: Vegetable: 2, Bread: 2, Meat: 3, Fat: 2

Greek Spinach and Feta Pie

⅓ cup butter, melted and
    divided
2 eggs
1 package (10 ounces)
    frozen chopped
    spinach, thawed and
    squeezed dry
1 container (15 ounces)
    ricotta cheese

1 package (4 ounces)
    crumbled feta cheese
¾ teaspoon finely grated
    lemon peel
¼ teaspoon black pepper
⅛ teaspoon ground nutmeg
1 package (16 ounces)
    frozen phyllo dough,
    thawed

PREHEAT oven to 350°F. Brush 13×9-inch baking dish lightly with butter.

BEAT eggs in medium bowl. Stir in spinach, ricotta cheese, feta cheese, lemon peel, pepper and nutmeg. Set aside.

CUT 8 sheets of phyllo dough in half crosswise, forming 16 rectangles about 13×8½ inches each. Cover dough with damp cloth or plastic wrap while assembling pie. Reserve remaining dough for another use.

PLACE 1 piece of dough in prepared dish; brush top lightly with butter. Top with another piece of dough and brush lightly with butter. Continue layering with 6 pieces of dough, brushing each piece lightly with butter. Spoon spinach mixture evenly over dough. Top spinach mixture with piece of dough; brush lightly with butter. Repeat layering with remaining 7 pieces of dough, brushing each piece lightly with butter.

BAKE, uncovered, 35 to 40 minutes or until golden brown.

Makes 6 servings

Serving Suggestion: Serve with cantaloupe slices and cherries.

Nutrients per Serving: Calories: 525, Total Fat: 30 g, Protein: 20 g,
Carbohydrate: 45 g, Cholesterol: 151 mg, Sodium: 795 mg, Dietary Fiber: trace
Dietary Exchanges: Vegetable: 1, Bread: 2½, Meat: 2, Fat: 4½

Baked Tomato Risotto

2 medium zucchini
1 jar (28 ounces) spaghetti
    sauce
1 can (14 ounces) chicken
    broth
1 can (4 ounces) sliced
    mushrooms

1 cup arborio rice
2 cups (8 ounces) shredded
    mozzarella cheese
    Yellow bell pepper slices
    (optional)

PREHEAT oven to 350°F. Spray 3-quart oval casserole with nonstick cooking spray.

CUT zucchini lengthwise in half. Cut crosswise into ¼-inch-thick slices. Combine spaghetti sauce, broth, zucchini, mushrooms and rice in prepared dish.

BAKE, covered, 30 minutes. Remove from oven and stir casserole. Cover and bake 15 to 20 minutes or until rice is tender. Remove from oven; sprinkle evenly with cheese. Bake, uncovered, 5 minutes or until cheese is melted. Garnish with yellow pepper, if desired.

Makes 6 servings

Nutrients per Serving: Calories: 350, Total Fat: 9 g, Protein: 15 g, Carbohydrate: 51 g, Cholesterol: 27 mg, Sodium: 977 mg, Dietary Fiber: 1 g Dietary Exchanges: Vegetable: 2, Bread: 2½, Meat: 1½, Fat: ½

Arborio is an Italian-grown short-grain rice that has large, plump grains. It is used in risotto dishes because its high starch content produces a creamy texture and it can absorb more liquid than long-grain rice.

Italian Three-Cheese Macaroni

2 cups uncooked elbow
   macaroni
4 tablespoons margarine or
   butter
3 tablespoons all-purpose
   flour
1 teaspoon dried Italian
   seasoning
½ to 1 teaspoon black
   pepper
½ teaspoon salt
2 cups milk

¾ cup (3 ounces) shredded
   Cheddar cheese
¼ cup grated Parmesan
   cheese
1 can (14½ ounces) diced
   tomatoes, drained
1 cup (4 ounces) shredded
   mozzarella cheese
½ cup dry bread crumbs
   Fresh chives and oregano
   sprig (optional)

PREHEAT oven to 350°F. Spray 2-quart round casserole with nonstick cooking spray.

COOK pasta according to package directions until al dente. Drain and set aside.

Meanwhile, **MELT** margarine in medium saucepan over medium heat. Add flour, Italian seasoning, pepper and salt, stirring until smooth. Gradually add milk, stirring constantly until slightly thickened. Add Cheddar and Parmesan cheeses; stir until cheeses melt.

LAYER pasta, tomatoes and cheese sauce in prepared dish. Repeat layers.

COMBINE mozzarella cheese and bread crumbs in small bowl. Sprinkle evenly over casserole. Spray bread crumb mixture several times with cooking spray.

BAKE, covered, 30 minutes or until hot and bubbly. Uncover and bake 5 minutes or until top is golden brown. Garnish with chives and oregano, if desired.   *Makes 4 servings*

Nutrients per Serving: Calories: 621, Total Fat: 26 g, Protein: 29 g, Carbohydrate: 67 g, Cholesterol: 41 mg, Sodium: 1303 mg, Dietary Fiber: trace Dietary Exchanges: Milk: ½, Vegetable: 2, Bread: 3½, Meat: 2, Fat: 3½

Spinach-Cheese Pasta Casserole

8 ounces uncooked pasta shells

2 eggs

1 cup ricotta cheese

1 jar (26 ounces) marinara sauce

1 teaspoon salt

1 package (10 ounces) frozen chopped spinach, thawed and squeezed dry

1 cup (4 ounces) shredded mozzarella cheese

¼ cup grated Parmesan cheese

PREHEAT oven to 350°F. Spray 1½-quart round casserole with nonstick cooking spray.

COOK pasta according to package directions until al dente. Drain.

Meanwhile, **WHISK** eggs in large bowl until blended. Add ricotta cheese; stir until combined. Stir pasta, marinara sauce and salt in large bowl until pasta is well coated. Pour pasta mixture into prepared dish. Top with ricotta mixture and spinach. Sprinkle mozzarella and Parmesan cheeses evenly over casserole.

BAKE, covered, 30 minutes. Uncover and bake 15 minutes or until hot and bubbly.   *Makes 6 to 8 servings*

Nutrients per Serving: Calories: 392, Total Fat: 16 g, Protein: 21 g, Carbohydrate: 40 g, Cholesterol: 106 mg, Sodium: 1072 mg, Dietary Fiber: 2 g Dietary Exchanges: Vegetable: 2, Bread: 2, Meat: 2, Fat: 2

Potatoes au Gratin

1½ pounds small red
  potatoes
 6 tablespoons margarine or
  butter, divided
 3 tablespoons all-purpose
  flour
 ½ teaspoon salt
 ¼ teaspoon ground white
  pepper

1½ cups milk
 1 cup (4 ounces) shredded
  Cheddar cheese
 4 green onions, thinly
  sliced
 ¾ cup cracker crumbs

PREHEAT oven to 350°F. Spray 1-quart round casserole with nonstick cooking spray.

PLACE potatoes in 2-quart saucepan; add enough water to cover potatoes. Bring to a boil over high heat. Cook, uncovered, about 10 minutes or until partially done. *Potatoes should still be firm in center.* Drain and rinse in cold water until potatoes are cool. Drain and set aside.

Meanwhile, **MELT** 4 tablespoons margarine in medium saucepan over medium heat. Add flour, salt and pepper, stirring until smooth. Gradually add milk, stirring constantly until sauce is thickened. Add cheese, stirring until cheese is melted.

CUT potatoes crosswise into ¼-inch-thick slices. Layer one third of potatoes in prepared dish. Top with one third of onions and one third of cheese sauce. Repeat layers twice, ending with cheese sauce.

MELT remaining 2 tablespoons margarine. Combine cracker crumbs and margarine in small bowl. Sprinkle evenly over casserole.

BAKE, uncovered, 35 to 40 minutes or until hot and bubbly and potatoes are tender. *Makes 4 to 6 servings*

Nutrients per Serving: Calories: 634, Total Fat: 24 g, Protein: 18 g, Carbohydrate: 87 g, Cholesterol: 22 mg, Sodium: 708 mg, Dietary Fiber: trace Dietary Exchanges: Bread: 6, Fat: 4½

Menu

Roast Beef

Potatoes au Gratin

Steamed Broccoli

Assorted Rolls

Apple Crisp with
Vanilla Ice Cream

Green Beans with Blue Cheese and Roasted Red Peppers

· ·

1 bag (20 ounces) frozen
    cut green beans
½ jar roasted red pepper
    strips (about 3 ounces),
    drained and slivered
⅛ teaspoon salt
⅛ teaspoon ground white
    pepper
4 ounces cream cheese
½ cup milk

¾ cup (3 ounces) blue
    cheese, crumbled
½ cup Italian-style bread
    crumbs
1 tablespoon margarine or
    butter, melted
Red and yellow bell
    pepper rose and fresh
    Italian parsley
    (optional)

PREHEAT oven to 350°F. Spray 2-quart oval casserole with nonstick cooking spray.

COMBINE green beans, red pepper strips, salt and white pepper in prepared dish.

PLACE cream cheese and milk in small saucepan; heat over low heat, stirring until melted. Add blue cheese; stir only until combined. Pour cheese mixture over green bean mixture and stir until green beans are coated.

COMBINE bread crumbs and margarine in small bowl; sprinkle evenly over casserole.

BAKE, uncovered, 20 minutes or until hot and bubbly. Garnish with bell peppers and Italian parsley, if desired.   *Makes 4 servings*

Nutrients per Serving: Calories: 297, Total Fat: 20 g, Protein: 11 g, Carbohydrate: 20 g, Cholesterol: 49 mg, Sodium: 906 mg, Dietary Fiber: 1 g Dietary Exchanges: Vegetable: 2, Bread: ½, Meat: 1, Fat: 3½

Easy Home Cooking

™

SLOW COOKER
Recipes

COME HOME TO COMFORT FOODS

Slow Cooker Recipes

Appetizers & Beverages

Caponata

1 medium eggplant (about 1 pound), peeled and cut into ½-inch pieces

1 can (14½ ounces) diced Italian plum tomatoes, undrained

1 medium onion, chopped

1 red bell pepper, cut into ½-inch pieces

½ cup prepared medium-hot salsa

¼ cup extra-virgin olive oil

2 tablespoons capers, drained

2 tablespoons balsamic vinegar

1 teaspoon dried oregano leaves

3 cloves garlic, minced

¼ teaspoon salt

⅓ cup packed fresh basil, cut into thin strips

Toasted sliced Italian or French bread

MIX all ingredients except basil and bread in slow cooker. Cover and cook on LOW 7 to 8 hours or until vegetables are crisp-tender. Stir in basil. Serve at room temperature with toasted bread.

Makes about 5¼ cups

Nutrients per Serving: Calories 42, Total Fat 3 g, Protein <1 g, Carbohydrate 4 g, Cholesterol 0 mg, Sodium 141 mg, Dietary Fiber <1 g
Dietary Exchanges: 1 Vegetable, ½ Fat

Mulled Apple Cider

2 quarts bottled apple cider
　　or juice (not unfiltered)
¼ cup packed brown sugar
1 square (8 inches) double-
　　thickness cheesecloth
8 allspice berries

4 cinnamon sticks, broken
　　into halves
12 whole cloves
1 large orange
　　Additional cinnamon
　　sticks (optional)

COMBINE apple cider and brown sugar in slow cooker. Rinse cheesecloth; squeeze out water. Wrap allspice berries and cinnamon stick halves in cheesecloth; tie securely with cotton string or strip of cheesecloth. Stick cloves randomly into orange; cut orange into quarters. Place spice bag and orange quarters in juice mixture. Cover and cook on HIGH 2½ to 3 hours. Once cooked, cider may be turned to LOW and kept warm up to 3 additional hours. Discard spice bag and orange quarters; ladle cider into mugs. Garnish with additional cinnamon sticks, if desired.　　*Makes 10 servings*

Nutrients per Serving: Calories 120, Total Fat <1 g, Protein <1 g, Carbohydrate 33 g, Cholesterol 0 mg, Sodium 8 mg, Dietary Fiber <1 g
Dietary Exchanges: 2 Fruit

KITCHEN HOW–TO

To make inserting cloves into the orange a little easier, first pierce the orange skin with point of wooden skewer. Remove the skewer and insert a clove.

Chili con Queso

1 pound pasteurized
   process cheese spread,
   cut into cubes
1 can (10 ounces) diced
   tomatoes and green
   chilies, undrained
1 cup sliced green onions
2 teaspoons ground
   coriander

2 teaspoons ground cumin
¾ teaspoon hot pepper
   sauce
Green onion strips
   (optional)
Hot pepper slices
   (optional)

COMBINE all ingredients except green onion strips and hot pepper slices in slow cooker until well blended. Cover and cook on LOW 2 to 3 hours or until hot.* Garnish with green onion strips and hot pepper slices, if desired.   *Makes 3 cups*

*Chili will be very hot; use caution when serving.

Nutrients per Serving: *Calories 233, Total Fat 16 g, Protein 13 g, Carbohydrate 10 g, Cholesterol 43 mg, Sodium 1208 mg, Dietary Fiber <1 g Dietary Exchanges: 2 Vegetable, 1½ Meat, 2 Fat*

Serve Chili con Queso with tortilla chips. Or, for something different, cut pita bread into triangles and toast in preheated 400°F oven for 5 minutes or until crisp.

Mocha Supreme

2 quarts brewed strong
  coffee
½ cup instant hot chocolate
  beverage mix
1 cinnamon stick, broken
  into halves

1 cup whipping cream
1 tablespoon powdered
  sugar

PLACE coffee, hot chocolate mix and cinnamon stick halves in slow cooker; stir. Cover and cook on HIGH 2 to 2½ hours or until hot. Remove and discard cinnamon stick halves.

BEAT cream in medium bowl with electric mixer on high speed until soft peaks form. Add powdered sugar; beat until stiff peaks form. Ladle hot beverage into mugs; top with whipped cream.

Makes 8 servings

Nutrients per Serving: *Calories 132, Total Fat 12 g, Protein 1 g, Carbohydrate 7 g, Cholesterol 41 mg, Sodium 51 mg, Dietary Fiber <1 g Dietary Exchanges: ½ Bread, 2 Fat*

You can whip cream faster if you first chill the beaters and bowl in the freezer for 15 minutes.

Barbecued Meatballs

2 pounds lean ground beef
1⅓ cups ketchup, divided
3 tablespoons seasoned
    dry bread crumbs
1 egg, slightly beaten
2 tablespoons dried onion
    flakes
¾ teaspoon garlic salt
½ teaspoon black pepper
1 cup packed brown sugar

1 can (6 ounces) tomato
    paste
¼ cup reduced-sodium soy
    sauce
¼ cup cider vinegar
1½ teaspoons hot pepper
    sauce
Diced bell peppers
    (optional)

PREHEAT oven to 350°F. Combine ground beef, ⅓ cup ketchup, bread crumbs, egg, onion flakes, garlic salt and black pepper in medium bowl. Mix lightly but thoroughly; shape into 1-inch meatballs. Place meatballs in two 15×10-inch jelly-roll pans or shallow roasting pans. Bake 18 minutes or until browned. Transfer meatballs to slow cooker.

MIX remaining 1 cup ketchup, sugar, tomato paste, soy sauce, vinegar and hot pepper sauce in medium bowl. Pour over meatballs. Cover and cook on LOW 4 hours. Serve with cocktail picks. Garnish with bell peppers, if desired.   *Makes about 4 dozen meatballs*

Variation: For Barbecued Franks, arrange 2 (12-ounce) packages or 3 (8-ounce) packages cocktail franks in slow cooker. Combine 1 cup ketchup, sugar, tomato paste, soy sauce, vinegar and hot pepper sauce in medium bowl; pour over franks. Cook according to directions for Barbecued Meatballs.

Nutrients per Serving: Calories 139, Total Fat 5 g, Protein 8 g, Carbohydrate 16 g, Cholesterol 32 mg, Sodium 441 mg, Dietary Fiber <1 g Dietary Exchanges: 1 Bread, 1 Meat, ½ Fat

Mulled Wine

....

2 bottles (750 ml each) dry
   red wine, such as
   Cabernet Sauvignon
1 cup light corn syrup
1 cup water
1 square (8 inches) double-
   thickness cheesecloth

Peel of 1 large orange
1 cinnamon stick, broken
   into halves
8 whole cloves
1 whole nutmeg
   Orange slices (optional)

COMBINE wine, corn syrup and water in slow cooker. Rinse
cheesecloth; squeeze out water. Wrap orange peel, cinnamon stick
halves, cloves and nutmeg in cheesecloth. Tie securely with cotton
string or strip of cheesecloth. Add to slow cooker. Cover and cook on
HIGH 2 to 2½ hours. Discard spice bag; ladle into glasses. Garnish
with orange slices, if desired.   *Makes 12 servings*

*Nutrients per Serving: Calories 179, Total Fat <1 g, Protein <1 g,
Carbohydrate 23 g, Cholesterol 0 mg, Sodium 31 mg, Dietary Fiber <1 g
Dietary Exchanges: 1½ Bread, 1½ Fat**

*Fat exchange accounts for the calories from the alcohol.

Main Courses

Southwest Turkey Tenderloin Stew

1 package (about
    1½ pounds) turkey
    tenderloins, cut into
    ¾-inch pieces
1 tablespoon chili powder
1 teaspoon ground cumin
¾ teaspoon salt
1 red bell pepper, cut into
    ¾-inch pieces
1 green bell pepper, cut into
    ¾-inch pieces
¾ cup chopped red or
    yellow onion

3 cloves garlic, minced
1 can (15½ ounces) chili
    beans in spicy sauce,
    undrained
1 can (14½ ounces) chili-
    style stewed tomatoes,
    undrained
¾ cup prepared salsa or
    picante sauce
    Fresh cilantro (optional)

PLACE turkey in slow cooker. Sprinkle chili powder, cumin and salt over turkey; toss to coat. Add red bell pepper, green bell pepper, onion, garlic, beans, tomatoes and salsa. Mix well. Cover and cook on LOW 5 hours or until turkey is no longer pink in centers and vegetables are crisp-tender. Ladle into bowls. Garnish with cilantro, if desired. *Makes 6 servings*

Nutrients per Serving: Calories 228, Total Fat 4 g, Protein 25 g, Carbohydrate 27 g, Cholesterol 44 mg, Sodium 943 mg, Dietary Fiber 4 g Dietary Exchanges: 2 Vegetable, 1 Bread, 2 Meat

Spareribs Simmered in Orange Sauce

4 pounds country-style
   pork spareribs
2 tablespoons vegetable oil
2 medium white onions, cut
   into ¼-inch slices
1 to 2 tablespoons dried
   ancho chilies, seeded
   and finely chopped
½ teaspoon ground
   cinnamon
¼ teaspoon ground cloves
1 can (16 ounces)
   tomatoes, undrained

2 cloves garlic
½ cup orange juice
⅓ cup dry white wine
⅓ cup packed brown sugar
1 teaspoon shredded
   orange peel
½ teaspoon salt
1 to 2 tablespoons cider
   vinegar
   Orange wedges (optional)

TRIM excess fat from ribs. Cut into individual riblets. Heat oil in large skillet over medium heat. Add ribs; cook 10 minutes or until browned on all sides. Remove to plate. Remove and discard all but 2 tablespoons drippings from skillet. Add onions, chilies, cinnamon and ground cloves. Cook and stir 4 minutes or until softened. Transfer onion mixture to slow cooker.

PROCESS tomatoes with juices and garlic in food processor or blender until smooth.

COMBINE tomato mixture, orange juice, wine, sugar, orange peel and salt in slow cooker. Add ribs; stir to coat. Cover and cook on LOW 5 hours or until ribs are fork-tender. Remove ribs to plates. Ladle out liquid to medium bowl. Let stand 5 minutes. Skim and discard fat. Stir in vinegar; serve over ribs. Serve with carrots and garnish with orange wedges, if desired.   *Makes 4 to 6 servings*

Nutrients per Serving: Calories 733, Total Fat 37 g, Protein 62 g, Carbohydrate 33 g, Cholesterol 125 mg, Sodium 575 mg, Dietary Fiber 3 g Dietary Exchanges: 2 Vegetable, ½ Fruit, 1 Bread, 9 Meat, 2 Fat

Bean Ragoût with Cilantro-Cornmeal Dumplings

2 cans (14½ ounces each) tomatoes, chopped and juice reserved
1½ cups chopped red bell pepper
1 large onion, chopped
1 can (15½ ounces) pinto or kidney beans, rinsed and drained
1 can (15½ ounces) black beans, rinsed and drained
2 small zucchini, sliced
½ cup chopped green bell pepper
½ cup chopped celery
1 poblano chili pepper,* seeded and chopped

2 cloves garlic, minced
3 tablespoons chili powder
2 teaspoons ground cumin
1 teaspoon dried oregano leaves
½ teaspoon salt, divided
⅛ teaspoon black pepper
¼ cup all-purpose flour
¼ cup yellow cornmeal
½ teaspoon baking powder
1 tablespoon vegetable shortening
2 tablespoons shredded Cheddar cheese
2 teaspoons minced fresh cilantro
¼ cup milk

COMBINE tomatoes with juice, red bell pepper, onion, beans, zucchini, green bell pepper, celery, poblano pepper, garlic, chili powder, cumin, oregano, ¼ teaspoon salt and black pepper in slow cooker; mix well. Cover and cook on LOW 7 to 8 hours.

PREPARE dumplings 1 hour before serving. Mix flour, cornmeal, baking powder and remaining ¼ teaspoon salt in medium bowl. Cut in shortening with pastry blender or two knives until mixture resembles coarse crumbs. Stir in cheese and cilantro. Pour milk into flour mixture. Blend just until dry ingredients are moistened. Turn slow cooker to HIGH. Drop dumplings by level tablespoonfuls (larger dumplings will not cook properly) on top of ragoût. Cover and cook 1 hour or until toothpick inserted in dumpling comes out clean.

Makes 6 servings

*Chili peppers can sting and irritate the skin; wear rubber gloves when handling peppers and do not touch eyes.

Nutrients per Serving: Calories 294, Total Fat 6 g, Protein 17 g, Carbohydrate 54 g, Cholesterol 3 mg, Sodium 998 mg, Dietary Fiber 10 g
Dietary Exchanges: 2 Vegetable, 3 Bread, ½ Fat

Texas-Style Barbecued Brisket

1 beef brisket (3 to 4 pounds), cut into halves, if necessary, to fit slow cooker
3 tablespoons Worcestershire sauce
1 tablespoon chili powder
1 teaspoon celery salt
1 teaspoon black pepper
1 teaspoon liquid smoke
2 cloves garlic, minced
2 bay leaves
Barbecue Sauce (recipe follows)

TRIM excess fat from meat and discard. Place meat in resealable plastic food storage bag. Combine Worcestershire sauce, chili powder, celery salt, pepper, liquid smoke, garlic and bay leaves in small bowl. Spread mixture on all sides of meat; seal bag. Refrigerate 24 hours.

PLACE meat and marinade in slow cooker. Cover and cook on LOW 7 hours. *Meanwhile,* prepare Barbecue Sauce.

REMOVE meat from slow cooker and pour juices into 2-cup measure; let stand 5 minutes. Skim fat from juices. Remove and discard bay leaves. Stir 1 cup of defatted juices into Barbecue Sauce. Discard remaining juices. Return meat and Barbecue Sauce to slow cooker. Cover and cook 1 hour or until meat is fork-tender. Remove meat to cutting board. Cut across grain into ¼-inch-thick slices. Serve 2 to 3 tablespoons Barbecue Sauce over each serving.

Makes 10 to 12 servings

Barbecue Sauce

2 tablespoons vegetable oil
1 medium onion, chopped
2 cloves garlic, minced
1 cup ketchup
½ cup molasses
¼ cup cider vinegar
2 teaspoons chili powder
½ teaspoon dry mustard

HEAT oil in medium saucepan over medium heat. Add onion and garlic; cook until onion is tender. Add remaining ingredients. Simmer 5 minutes.

Makes 2½ cups

Nutrients per Serving: Calories 275, Total Fat 11 g, Protein 24 g, Carbohydrate 20 g, Cholesterol 73 mg, Sodium 658 mg, Dietary Fiber 1 g Dietary Exchanges: 1½ Bread, 3½ Meat

Pork Stew

· ·

2 tablespoons vegetable oil, divided

3 pounds fresh lean boneless pork butt, cut into 1½-inch cubes

2 medium white onions, thinly sliced

3 cloves garlic, minced

1 teaspoon salt

1 teaspoon ground cumin

¾ teaspoon dried oregano leaves

1 can (8 ounces) tomatillos, drained and chopped *or* 1 cup husked and chopped fresh tomatillos

1 can (4 ounces) chopped green chilies, drained

½ cup reduced-sodium chicken broth

1 large tomato, peeled and coarsely chopped

¼ cup fresh cilantro, chopped *or* ½ teaspoon ground coriander

2 teaspoons lime juice

4 cups hot cooked white rice

½ cup toasted slivered almonds (optional)

HEAT 1 tablespoon oil in large skillet over medium heat. Add pork; cook 10 minutes or until browned on all sides. Remove and set aside. Heat remaining 1 tablespoon oil in skillet. Add onions, garlic, salt, cumin and oregano; cook and stir 2 minutes or until soft.

COMBINE pork, onion mixture and remaining ingredients except rice and almonds in slow cooker; mix well. Cover and cook on LOW 5 hours or until pork is tender and barely pink in centers. Serve over rice and sprinkle with almonds, if desired.   *Makes 10 servings*

Nutrients per Serving: Calories 377, Total Fat 17 g, Protein 32 g, Carbohydrate 23 g, Cholesterol 76 mg, Sodium 357 mg, Dietary Fiber 1 g
Dietary Exchanges: 1½ Bread, 4½ Meat, ½ Fat

Lamb in Dill Sauce

2 large potatoes, peeled and cut into 1-inch cubes
½ cup chopped onion
1½ teaspoons salt
½ teaspoon black pepper
½ teaspoon dried dill weed *or* 4 sprigs fresh dill
1 bay leaf
2 pounds lean lamb stew meat, cut into 1-inch cubes
1 cup plus 3 tablespoons water, divided
2 tablespoons all-purpose flour
1 teaspoon sugar
2 tablespoons lemon juice
Fresh dill (optional)

LAYER ingredients in slow cooker in the following order: potatoes, onion, salt, pepper, dill weed, bay leaf, lamb and 1 cup water. Cover and cook on LOW 6 to 8 hours.

REMOVE lamb and potatoes with slotted spoon; cover and keep warm. Remove and discard bay leaf. Turn heat to HIGH. Stir flour and remaining 3 tablespoons water in small bowl until smooth. Add half of cooking juices and sugar. Mix well and return to slow cooker. Cover and cook 15 minutes. Stir in lemon juice. Return lamb and potatoes to slow cooker. Cover and cook 10 minutes or until heated through. Garnish with fresh dill, if desired.   *Makes 6 servings*

Nutrients per Serving: Calories 299, Total Fat 11 g, Protein 33 g, Carbohydrate 15 g, Cholesterol 108 mg, Sodium 649 mg, Dietary Fiber 1 g
Dietary Exchanges: 1 Bread, 4 Meat

K I T C H E N   H O W – T O

Here's an easy way to mince fresh herbs. Put the herbs in a measuring cup. Place the point of kitchen scissors in the cup and snip until finely chopped.

Garden Vegetable Tabbouleh Stew

1 large onion, chopped
2 medium carrots, cut lengthwise into halves, then cut into 1-inch pieces
1 cup green beans, cut into 1-inch pieces
2 medium green onions, thinly sliced
1 small zucchini (4 ounces), sliced
1 can (15½ ounces) chick-peas (garbanzo beans), rinsed and drained

2 cans (14½ ounces each) diced tomatoes, undrained
¼ teaspoon salt
⅛ teaspoon black pepper
1 box (6 to 7 ounces) tabbouleh mix
1½ cups water
¼ cup olive oil
Sour cream (optional)
Fresh mint (optional)

LAYER ingredients in slow cooker in the following order: onion, carrots, green beans, green onions, zucchini, chick-peas, tomatoes with juice, salt and pepper. Sprinkle tabbouleh mix over vegetables. Pour water and olive oil evenly over top. Cover and cook on LOW 6 to 8 hours or until vegetables are crisp-tender. Serve in bowls and garnish with sour cream and fresh mint, if desired.

Makes 4 servings

Nutrients per Serving: Calories 448, Total Fat 16 g, Protein 13 g, Carbohydrate 66 g, Cholesterol 0 mg, Sodium 1427 mg, Dietary Fiber 10 g
Dietary Exchanges: 4 Vegetable, 3 Bread, 3 Fat

Thai Turkey & Noodles

1 package (about
    1½ pounds) turkey
    tenderloins, cut into
    ¾-inch pieces
1 red bell pepper, cut into
    short, thin strips
1¼ cups reduced-sodium
    chicken broth, divided
¼ cup reduced-sodium soy
    sauce
3 cloves garlic, minced
¾ teaspoon crushed red
    pepper flakes

¼ teaspoon salt
2 tablespoons cornstarch
3 green onions, cut into
    ½-inch pieces
⅓ cup creamy or chunky
    peanut butter (not
    natural-style)
12 ounces hot cooked
    vermicelli pasta
¾ cup peanuts or cashews,
    chopped
¾ cup cilantro, chopped

PLACE turkey, bell pepper, 1 cup broth, soy sauce, garlic, red pepper flakes and salt in slow cooker. Cover and cook on LOW 3 hours.

MIX cornstarch with remaining ¼ cup broth in small bowl until smooth. Turn slow cooker to HIGH. Stir in green onions, peanut butter and cornstarch mixture. Cover and cook 30 minutes or until sauce is thickened and turkey is no longer pink in centers. Stir well. Serve over vermicelli. Sprinkle with peanuts and cilantro.

Makes 6 servings

Nutrients per Serving: Calories 387, Total Fat 19 g, Protein 31 g, Carbohydrate 25 g, Cholesterol 44 mg, Sodium 1044 mg, Dietary Fiber 3 g
Dietary Exchanges: 1½ Bread, 3½ Meat, 2 Fat

Cook's Nook

If you don't have vermicelli on hand, try substituting ramen noodles. Discard the flavor packet from ramen soup mix and drop the noodles into boiling water. Cook the noodles 2 to 3 minutes or until just tender. Drain and serve hot.

Favorite Beef Stew

3 carrots, cut lengthwise into halves, then cut into 1-inch pieces
3 ribs celery, cut into 1-inch pieces
2 large potatoes, peeled and cut into ½-inch pieces
1½ cups chopped onions
3 cloves garlic, chopped
1 bay leaf
1½ tablespoons Worcestershire sauce
¾ teaspoon dried thyme leaves
¾ teaspoon dried basil leaves
½ teaspoon black pepper
2 pounds lean beef stew meat, cut into 1-inch pieces
1 can (14½ ounces) diced tomatoes, undrained
1 can (14½ ounces) reduced-sodium beef broth
¼ cup all-purpose flour
½ cup cold water

LAYER ingredients in slow cooker in the following order: carrots, celery, potatoes, onions, garlic, bay leaf, Worcestershire sauce, thyme, basil, pepper, beef, tomatoes with juice and broth. Cover and cook on LOW 8 to 9 hours.

REMOVE beef and vegetables to large serving bowl; cover and keep warm. Remove and discard bay leaf. Turn slow cooker to HIGH; cover. Mix flour and water in small bowl until smooth. Add ½ cup cooking liquid; mix well. Stir flour mixture into slow cooker. Cover and cook 15 minutes or until thickened. Pour sauce over beef and vegetables. Serve immediately.　　*Makes 6 to 8 servings*

Nutrients per Serving: Calories 364, Total Fat 8 g, Protein 43 g, Carbohydrate 29 g, Cholesterol 95 mg, Sodium 279 mg, Dietary Fiber 3 g
Dietary Exchanges: 2 Vegetable, 1 Bread, 4½ Meat

Pork Chops with Jalapeño-Pecan Cornbread Stuffing

6 boneless loin pork chops,
    1 inch thick
    (1½ pounds)
¾ cup chopped onion
¾ cup chopped celery
½ cup coarsely chopped
    pecans
½ medium jalapeño pepper,*
    seeded and chopped

1 teaspoon rubbed sage
½ teaspoon dried rosemary
    leaves
⅛ teaspoon black pepper
4 cups unseasoned
    cornbread stuffing mix
1¼ cups reduced-sodium
    chicken broth
1 egg, lightly beaten

TRIM excess fat from pork and discard. Spray large skillet with nonstick cooking spray; heat over medium heat. Add pork; cook 10 minutes or until browned on all sides. Remove; set aside. Add onion, celery, pecans, jalapeño pepper, sage, rosemary and black pepper to skillet. Cook 5 minutes or until tender; set aside.

COMBINE cornbread stuffing mix, vegetable mixture and broth in medium bowl. Stir in egg. Spoon stuffing mixture into slow cooker. Arrange pork on top. Cover and cook on LOW about 5 hours or until pork is tender and barely pink in centers. Serve with vegetable salad, if desired.   *Makes 6 servings*

*Jalapeño peppers can sting and irritate the skin; wear rubber gloves when handling peppers and do not touch eyes.

Tip: If you prefer a more moist dressing, increase the chicken broth to 1½ cups.

Nutrients per Serving: Calories 272, Total Fat 14 g, Protein 17 g, Carbohydrate 19 g, Cholesterol 75 mg, Sodium 380 mg, Dietary Fiber 1 g Dietary Exchanges: 1 Vegetable, 1 Bread, 2 Meat, 1½ Fat

Coq au Vin

4 thick slices bacon
2 cups frozen pearl onions, thawed
1 cup sliced button mushrooms
1 clove garlic, minced
1 teaspoon dried thyme leaves
⅛ teaspoon black pepper
6 boneless skinless chicken breast halves (about 2 pounds)

½ cup dry red wine
¾ cup reduced-sodium chicken broth
¼ cup tomato paste
3 tablespoons all-purpose flour
Hot cooked egg noodles (optional)

COOK bacon in medium skillet over medium heat. Drain and crumble. Layer ingredients in slow cooker in the following order: onions, bacon, mushrooms, garlic, thyme, pepper, chicken, wine and broth. Cover and cook on LOW 6 to 8 hours.

REMOVE chicken and vegetables; cover and keep warm. Ladle ½ cup cooking liquid into small bowl; allow to cool slightly. Turn slow cooker to HIGH; cover. Mix reserved liquid, tomato paste and flour until smooth. Return mixture to slow cooker; cover and cook 15 minutes or until thickened. Serve over egg noodles, if desired.

Makes 6 servings

Nutrients per Serving: *Calories 283, Total Fat 6 g, Protein 37 g, Carbohydrate 15 g, Cholesterol 96 mg, Sodium 295 mg, Dietary Fiber 1 g Dietary Exchanges: 3 Vegetable, 4 Meat*

Coq au Vin is a classic French dish that is made with bone-in chicken, salt pork or bacon, brandy, red wine and herbs. The dish originated when farmers needed a way to cook old chickens that could no longer breed. A slow, moist cooking method was needed to tenderize the tough old birds.

Menu

Coq au Vin

Garlic Mashed Potatoes

Sautéed Zucchini
and Tomatoes

Chocolate Angel
Food Cake

Chili Turkey Loaf

2 pounds ground turkey
1 cup chopped onion
⅔ cup Italian-style
    seasoned dry bread
    crumbs
½ cup chopped green bell
    pepper
½ cup chili sauce
4 cloves garlic, minced

2 eggs, lightly beaten
2 tablespoons horseradish
    mustard
1 teaspoon salt
½ teaspoon Italian
    seasoning
¼ teaspoon black pepper
    Prepared salsa (optional)

MAKE foil handles for loaf using technique on page 10. Mix all ingredients except salsa in large bowl. Shape into round loaf and place on top of foil strips. Transfer to bottom of slow cooker using foil handles. Cover and cook on LOW 4½ to 5 hours or until temperature is 170°F. Remove loaf from slow cooker using foil handles. Place on serving plate. Let stand 5 minutes before serving. Cut into wedges and top with salsa, if desired. Serve with steamed carrots, if desired.

Makes 8 servings

Nutrients per Serving: Calories 263, Total Fat 13 g, Protein 23 g, Carbohydrate 12 g, Cholesterol 110 mg, Sodium 733 mg, Dietary Fiber 1 g
Dietary Exchanges: 1 Bread, 3 Meat, ½ Fat

Mediterranean Stew

1 medium butternut or acorn squash, peeled and cut into 1-inch cubes

2 cups unpeeled eggplant, cut into 1-inch cubes

2 cups sliced zucchini

1 can (15½ ounces) chick-peas (garbanzo beans), rinsed and drained

1 package (10 ounces) frozen cut okra

1 can (8 ounces) tomato sauce

1 cup chopped onion

1 medium tomato, chopped

1 medium carrot, thinly sliced

½ cup reduced-sodium vegetable broth

⅓ cup raisins

1 clove garlic, minced

½ teaspoon ground cumin

½ teaspoon ground turmeric

¼ to ½ teaspoon ground red pepper

¼ teaspoon ground cinnamon

¼ teaspoon paprika

6 to 8 cups hot cooked couscous or rice

Fresh parsley (optional)

COMBINE all ingredients except couscous and parsley in slow cooker; mix well. Cover and cook on LOW 8 to 10 hours or until vegetables are crisp-tender. Serve over couscous. Garnish with parsley, if desired.

Makes 6 servings

Nutrients per Serving: *Calories 377, Total Fat 2 g, Protein 14 g, Carbohydrate 78 g, Cholesterol 0 mg, Sodium 508 mg, Dietary Fiber 16 g Dietary Exchanges: 3 Vegetable, 4 Bread*

Butternut squash is a member of the winter squash family. It is low in calories, fat and sodium. Although all squash are a good source of beta-carotene, winter squash develops additional beta-carotene after it has been picked and stored.

Veggie Mac and Tuna

1½ cups (6 ounces) elbow
    macaroni, uncooked
3 tablespoons butter or
    margarine
1 small onion, chopped
½ medium red bell pepper,
    chopped
½ medium green bell
    pepper, chopped
¼ cup all-purpose flour

1¾ cups milk
8 ounces cubed light
    pasteurized process
    cheese product
½ teaspoon dried marjoram
    leaves
1 package (10 ounces)
    frozen peas
1 can (9 ounces) tuna in
    water, drained

COOK macaroni according to package directions until just tender;
drain. Melt butter in medium saucepan over medium heat. Add onion
and bell peppers. Cook and stir 5 minutes or until tender. Add flour.
Stir constantly over medium heat 2 minutes. Stir in milk and bring to
a boil. Boil, stirring constantly, until thickened. Reduce heat to low;
add cheese and marjoram. Stir until cheese is melted.

COMBINE macaroni, cheese sauce, peas and tuna in slow cooker.
Cover and cook on LOW 2½ hours or until bubbly at edge.

Makes 6 servings

Nutrients per Serving: Calories 446, Total Fat 20 g, Protein 29 g,
Carbohydrate 38 g, Cholesterol 69 mg, Sodium 821 mg, Dietary Fiber 3 g
Dietary Exchanges: 1 Vegetable, 2 Bread, 3 Meat, 2½ Fat

Yankee Pot Roast and Vegetables

1 beef chuck pot roast
   (2½ pounds)
3 medium baking potatoes
   (about 1 pound),
   unpeeled and cut into
   quarters
2 large carrots, cut into
   ¾-inch slices
2 ribs celery, cut into
   ¾-inch slices

1 medium onion, sliced
1 large parsnip, cut into
   ¾-inch slices
2 bay leaves
1 teaspoon dried rosemary
   leaves
½ teaspoon dried thyme
   leaves
½ cup reduced-sodium beef
   broth

TRIM excess fat from meat and discard. Cut into serving pieces; sprinkle with salt and pepper. Combine vegetables, bay leaves, rosemary and thyme in slow cooker. Place beef over vegetables in slow cooker. Pour broth over beef. Cover and cook on LOW 8½ to 9 hours or until beef is fork-tender. Remove beef to serving platter. Arrange vegetables around beef. Remove and discard bay leaves.

Makes 6 servings

Nutrients per Serving: Calories 494, Total Fat 17 g, Protein 48 g, Carbohydrate 35 g, Cholesterol 124 mg, Sodium 139 mg, Dietary Fiber 2 g
Dietary Exchanges: 1 Vegetable, 2 Bread, 6 Meat

To make gravy, ladle the juice into a 2-cup measure; let stand 5 minutes. Skim off and discard the fat. Measure remaining juice and heat to a boil in small saucepan. For each cup of juice, mix 2 tablespoons of flour with ¼ cup of cold water until smooth. Stir flour mixture into boiling juice. Stir constantly 1 minute or until thickened.

Menu

Yankee Pot Roast and Vegetables

Tossed Green Salad

Boston Brown Bread
(page 154)

Apple Pie

Lentil Stew over Couscous

1 large onion, chopped
1 green bell pepper,
   chopped
4 ribs celery, chopped
1 medium carrot, cut
   lengthwise into halves,
   then cut into 1-inch
   pieces
2 cloves garlic, chopped
3 cups lentils (1 pound),
   rinsed
1 can (14½ ounces) diced
   tomatoes, undrained

1 can (14½ ounces)
   reduced-sodium
   chicken broth
3 cups water
¼ teaspoon black pepper
1 teaspoon dried marjoram
   leaves
1 tablespoon cider vinegar
1 tablespoon olive oil
4½ to 5 cups hot cooked
   couscous
   Carrot curls (optional)
   Celery leaves (optional)

COMBINE onion, green bell pepper, celery, carrot, garlic, lentils, tomatoes with juice, broth, water, black pepper and marjoram in slow cooker. Stir; cover and cook on LOW 8 to 9 hours.

STIR in vinegar and olive oil. Serve over couscous. Garnish with carrot curls and celery leaves, if desired.   *Makes 12 servings*

Tip: Lentil stew keeps well in the refrigerator for up to one week. Stew can also be frozen in airtight container in freezer for up to three months.

Nutrients per Serving: Calories 203, Total Fat 2 g, Protein 11 g, Carbohydrate 37 g, Cholesterol 0 mg, Sodium 128 mg, Dietary Fiber 4 g Dietary Exchanges: 1 Vegetable, 2 Bread, ½ Meat

Forty-Clove Chicken

1 frying chicken
    (3 pounds), cut into
    serving pieces
1 to 2 tablespoons olive oil
¼ cup dry white wine
⅛ cup dry vermouth
2 tablespoons chopped
    fresh parsley *or*
    2 teaspoons dried
    parsley leaves
2 teaspoons dried basil
    leaves

1 teaspoon dried oregano
    leaves
    Pinch of crushed red
    pepper flakes
40 cloves garlic (about
    2 heads), peeled
4 ribs celery, sliced
    Juice and peel of 1 lemon
    Fresh herbs (optional)

REMOVE skin from chicken, if desired. Sprinkle with salt and pepper. Heat oil in large skillet over medium heat. Add chicken; cook 10 minutes or until browned on all sides. Remove to platter.

COMBINE wine, vermouth, parsley, basil, oregano and red pepper flakes in large bowl. Add garlic and celery; coat well. Transfer garlic and celery to slow cooker with slotted spoon. Add chicken to herb mixture; coat well. Place chicken on top of vegetables in slow cooker. Sprinkle lemon juice and peel in slow cooker; add remaining herb mixture. Cover and cook on LOW 6 hours or until chicken is no longer pink in centers. Garnish with fresh herbs, if desired.

Makes 4 to 6 servings

Nutrients per Serving: Calories 416, Total Fat 20 g, Protein 41 g, Carbohydrate 14 g, Cholesterol 139 mg, Sodium 173 mg, Dietary Fiber 1 g
Dietary Exchanges: 2 Vegetable, 6 Meat, ½ Fat

Peeling 40 cloves of garlic is easy if you first separate the cloves from the head and then drop them into boiling water for 30 seconds. Drain, wait until the garlic is cool to the touch and slip the peels off with your fingers.

Soups & Side Dishes

Green Beans with Savory Mushroom Sauce

2 packages (10 ounces
    each) frozen French-
    style green beans,
    thawed
1 can (10¾ ounces)
    condensed cream of
    mushroom soup,
    undiluted
¼ cup dry vermouth or dry
    white wine

4 ounces (1½ cups) fresh
    mushrooms, sliced
½ teaspoon salt
½ teaspoon dried thyme
    leaves
¼ teaspoon black pepper
1 cup crushed prepared
    croutons or canned
    fried onion rings

COMBINE all ingredients except croutons in slow cooker. Mix until well blended. Cover and cook on LOW 3 to 4 hours or until beans are crisp-tender. Sprinkle with croutons. Serve warm.

Makes 6 to 8 servings

Nutrients per Serving: Calories 159, Total Fat 5 g, Protein 5 g, Carbohydrate 22 g, Cholesterol 25 mg, Sodium 717 mg, Dietary Fiber < 1 g Dietary Exchanges: 2 Vegetable, 1 Bread, 1 Fat

Russian Borscht

4 cups thinly sliced green
    cabbage
1½ pounds fresh beets,
    shredded
5 small carrots, peeled, cut
    lengthwise into halves,
    then cut into 1-inch
    pieces
1 parsnip, peeled, cut
    lengthwise into halves,
    then cut into 1-inch
    pieces
1 cup chopped onion
4 cloves garlic, minced

1 pound lean beef stew
    meat, cut into ½-inch
    cubes
1 can (14½ ounces) diced
    tomatoes, undrained
3 cans (14½ ounces each)
    reduced-sodium beef
    broth
¼ cup lemon juice
1 tablespoon sugar
1 teaspoon black pepper
    Sour cream (optional)
    Fresh parsley (optional)

LAYER ingredients in slow cooker in the following order: cabbage, beets, carrots, parsnip, onion, garlic, beef, tomatoes with juice, broth, lemon juice, sugar and pepper. Cover and cook on LOW 7 to 9 hours or until vegetables are crisp-tender. Season with additional lemon juice and sugar, if desired. Dollop with sour cream and garnish with parsley, if desired.   *Makes 12 servings*

Nutrients per Serving: Calories 128, Total Fat 2 g, Protein 13 g, Carbohydrate 15 g, Cholesterol 24 mg, Sodium 146 mg, Dietary Fiber 2 g
Dietary Exchanges: 3 Vegetable, 1½ Meat

Instead of slicing the cabbage with a knife, you can shred it with the large shredder holes of a four-sided grater or in a food processor.

Bean Pot Medley

1 can (15½ ounces) black beans, rinsed and drained
1 can (15½ ounces) red beans, rinsed and drained
1 can (15½ ounces) Great Northern beans, rinsed and drained
1 can (15½ ounces) black-eyed peas, rinsed and drained
1 can (8½ ounces) baby lima beans, rinsed and drained

1½ cups ketchup
1 cup chopped onion
1 cup chopped red bell pepper
1 cup chopped green bell pepper
½ cup packed brown sugar
½ cup water
2 to 3 teaspoons cider vinegar
1 teaspoon dry mustard
2 bay leaves
⅛ teaspoon black pepper

COMBINE all ingredients in slow cooker; stir. Cover and cook on LOW 6 to 7 hours or until onion and peppers are tender. Remove and discard bay leaves. *Makes 8 servings*

Nutrients per Serving: Calories 375, Total Fat 4 g, Protein 19 g, Carbohydrate 77 g, Cholesterol 0 mg, Sodium 1132 mg, Dietary Fiber 12 g Dietary Exchanges: 5 Bread, ½ Fat

Mediterranean Gumbo

1 medium onion, chopped
½ medium green bell
   pepper, chopped
2 cloves garlic, minced
1 can (14½ ounces) whole
   tomatoes, undrained
   and coarsely chopped
2 cans (14½ ounces each)
   reduced-sodium
   chicken broth
1 can (8 ounces) tomato
   sauce
1 jar (2½ ounces) sliced
   mushrooms

¼ cup ripe olives, sliced
½ cup orange juice
½ cup dry white wine
   (optional)
2 bay leaves
1 teaspoon dried basil
   leaves
¼ teaspoon fennel seed,
   crushed
⅛ teaspoon black pepper
1 pound medium shrimp,
   peeled

PLACE all ingredients except shrimp in slow cooker. Cover and cook on LOW 4 to 4½ hours or until vegetables are crisp-tender. Stir in shrimp. Cover and cook 15 to 30 minutes or until shrimp are opaque. Remove and discard bay leaves. *Makes 6 servings*

Nutrients per Serving: Calories 144, Total Fat 3 g, Protein 17 g, Carbohydrate 12 g, Cholesterol 117 mg, Sodium 869 mg, Dietary Fiber 2 g
Dietary Exchanges: 1½ Vegetable, 1½ Meat

If you prefer a hearty soup, add more seafood. Cut 1 pound of whitefish or cod into 1-inch pieces. Add the fish to your slow cooker 45 minutes before serving. Cover and cook on LOW.

Rustic Potatoes au Gratin

½ cup milk
1 can (10¾ ounces) condensed Cheddar cheese soup, undiluted
1 package (8 ounces) cream cheese, softened
1 clove garlic, minced

¼ teaspoon ground nutmeg
⅛ teaspoon black pepper
2 pounds baking potatoes, cut into ¼-inch slices
1 small onion, thinly sliced
Paprika (optional)

HEAT milk in small saucepan over medium heat until small bubbles form around edge of pan. Remove from heat. Add soup, cheese, garlic, nutmeg and pepper. Stir until smooth. Layer ¼ of potatoes and onion on bottom of slow cooker. Top with ¼ of soup mixture. Repeat layers 3 times. Cover and cook on LOW 6½ to 7 hours or until potatoes are tender and most of liquid is absorbed. Sprinkle with paprika, if desired.   *Makes 6 servings*

Variation: Potatoes may be peeled, if desired.

Nutrients per Serving: Calories 421, Total Fat 17 g, Protein 10 g, Carbohydrate 59 g, Cholesterol 53 mg, Sodium 503 mg, Dietary Fiber <1 g Dietary Exchanges: 4 Bread, 3 Fat

Savory Pea Soup with Sausage

8 ounces smoked sausage, cut lengthwise into halves, then cut into ½-inch pieces

1 package (16 ounces) dried split peas, rinsed

3 medium carrots, sliced

2 ribs celery, sliced

1 medium onion, chopped

¾ teaspoon dried marjoram leaves

1 bay leaf

2 cans (14½ ounces each) reduced-sodium chicken broth

HEAT small skillet over medium heat. Add sausage; cook 5 to 8 minutes or until browned. Drain well. Combine sausage and remaining ingredients in slow cooker. Cover and cook on LOW 4 to 5 hours or until peas are tender. Turn off heat. Remove and discard bay leaf. Cover and let stand 15 minutes to thicken.

Makes 6 servings

Nutrients per Serving: *Calories 424, Total Fat 13 g, Protein 27 g, Carbohydrate 53 g, Cholesterol 26 mg, Sodium 585 mg, Dietary Fiber 5 g Dietary Exchanges: 1 Vegetable, 3 Bread, 2 Meat, 1½ Fat*

Cook's Nook

Wondering what type of sausage to use? Try kielbasa or chorizo. If you prefer, smoked ham would be a good sausage substitute.

Chicken and Vegetable Chowder

1 pound boneless skinless
  chicken breasts, cut
  into 1-inch pieces
10 ounces frozen broccoli
  cuts
1 cup sliced carrots
½ cup chopped onion
½ cup whole kernel corn
1 jar (4½ ounces) sliced
  mushrooms, drained

2 cloves garlic, minced
½ teaspoon dried thyme
  leaves
1 can (14½ ounces)
  reduced-sodium
  chicken broth
1 can (10¾ ounces)
  condensed cream of
  potato soup
⅓ cup half-and-half

COMBINE all ingredients except half-and-half in slow cooker. Cover and cook on LOW 5 hours or until vegetables are tender and chicken is no longer pink in centers. Stir in half-and-half. Turn to HIGH. Cover and cook 15 minutes or until heated through.   *Makes 6 servings*

Variation: If desired, ½ cup (2 ounces) shredded Swiss or Cheddar cheese can be added. Add to thickened broth, stirring over LOW heat until melted.

Nutrients per Serving: Calories 188, Total Fat 5 g, Protein 22 g, Carbohydrate 15 g, Cholesterol 54 mg, Sodium 704 mg, Dietary Fiber 2 g Dietary Exchanges: 1 Bread, 2 Meat

Risi Bisi

1½ cups converted long
    grain white rice
¾ cup chopped onion
2 cloves garlic, minced
2 cans (14½ ounces each)
    reduced-sodium
    chicken broth
⅓ cup water
¾ teaspoon Italian
    seasoning

½ teaspoon dried basil
    leaves
½ cup frozen peas, thawed
¼ cup grated Parmesan
    cheese
¼ cup toasted pine nuts
    (optional)

COMBINE rice, onion and garlic in slow cooker. Heat broth and water in small saucepan to a boil. Stir boiling liquid, Italian seasoning and basil into rice mixture. Cover and cook on LOW 2 to 3 hours or until liquid is absorbed. Add peas. Cover and cook 1 hour. Stir in cheese. Spoon rice into serving bowl. Sprinkle with pine nuts, if desired.

Makes 6 servings

Nutrients per Serving: Calories 222, Total Fat 2 g, Protein 9 g, Carbohydrate 42 g, Cholesterol 3 mg, Sodium 295 mg, Dietary Fiber 1 g
Dietary Exchanges: 3 Bread

Risi Bisi ("rice and peas") is a traditional Italian dish. It is said to be the first dish served each April 29th at the Venetian feasts honoring St. Mark. Small Italian peas are sweetest and most tender at that time of year.

Minestrone alla Milanese

2 cans (14½ ounces each) reduced-sodium beef broth
1 can (14½ ounces) diced tomatoes, undrained
1 cup diced potato
1 cup coarsely chopped green cabbage
1 cup coarsely chopped carrots
1 cup sliced zucchini
¾ cup chopped onion
¾ cup sliced fresh green beans
¾ cup coarsely chopped celery
¾ cup water
2 tablespoons olive oil
1 clove garlic, minced
½ teaspoon dried basil leaves
¼ teaspoon dried rosemary leaves
1 bay leaf
1 can (15½ ounces) cannellini beans, rinsed and drained
Grated Parmesan cheese (optional)

COMBINE all ingredients except cannellini beans and cheese in slow cooker; mix well. Cover and cook on LOW 5 to 6 hours. Add cannellini beans. Cover and cook on LOW 1 hour or until vegetables are crisp-tender. Remove and discard bay leaf. Garnish with cheese, if desired.   *Makes 8 to 10 servings*

Nutrients per Serving: Calories 135, Total Fat 4 g, Protein 8 g, Carbohydrate 23 g, Cholesterol 0 mg, Sodium 242 mg, Dietary Fiber 5 g
Dietary Exchanges: 1½ Vegetable, 1 Bread, ½ Fat

Orange-Spice Glazed Carrots

1 package (32 ounces)
   baby carrots
½ cup packed brown sugar
½ cup orange juice
3 tablespoons butter or
   margarine

¾ teaspoon ground
   cinnamon
¼ teaspoon ground nutmeg
2 tablespoons cornstarch
¼ cup water

COMBINE all ingredients except cornstarch and water in slow cooker. Cover and cook on LOW 3½ to 4 hours or until carrots are crisp-tender. Spoon carrots into serving bowl. Remove juices to small saucepan. Heat to a boil. Mix cornstarch and water in small bowl until blended. Stir into saucepan. Boil 1 minute or until thickened, stirring constantly. Pour over carrots.   *Makes 6 servings*

Nutrients per Serving: Calories 193, Total Fat 6 g, Protein 2 g, Carbohydrate 35 g, Cholesterol 15 mg, Sodium 153 mg, Dietary Fiber <1 g Dietary Exchanges: 2 Vegetable, 1½ Bread, 1 Fat

Navy Bean Bacon Chowder

1½ cups dried navy beans,
   rinsed
2 cups cold water
6 thick slices bacon
1 medium carrot, cut
   lengthwise into halves,
   then cut into 1-inch
   pieces
1 rib celery, chopped
1 medium onion, chopped

1 small turnip, cut into
   1-inch pieces
1 teaspoon dried Italian
   seasoning
⅛ teaspoon black pepper
1 large can (46 ounces)
   reduced-sodium
   chicken broth
1 cup milk

SOAK beans overnight in cold water.

COOK bacon in medium skillet over medium heat. Drain and crumble. Combine carrot, celery, onion, turnip, Italian seasoning, pepper, beans and bacon in slow cooker; mix slightly. Pour broth over top. Cover and cook on LOW 7½ to 9 hours or until beans are crisp-tender.

LADLE 2 cups of soup mixture into food processor or blender. Process until smooth; return to slow cooker. Add milk; cover and heat on HIGH 10 minutes or until heated through.   *Makes 6 servings*

Nutrients per Serving: Calories 270, Total Fat 5 g, Protein 20 g, Carbohydrate 39 g, Cholesterol 8 mg, Sodium 470 mg, Dietary Fiber 1 g
Dietary Exchanges: 1 Vegetable, 2 Bread, 1 Meat, 1 Fat

150

Breads & Desserts

Steamed Southern Sweet Potato Custard

1 can (16 ounces) cut sweet
   potatoes, drained
1 can (12 ounces)
   evaporated milk,
   divided
½ cup packed brown sugar
2 eggs, lightly beaten

1 teaspoon ground
   cinnamon
½ teaspoon ground ginger
¼ teaspoon salt
   Whipped cream (optional)
   Ground nutmeg (optional)

PROCESS sweet potatoes with about ¼ cup milk in food processor
or blender until smooth. Add remaining milk, brown sugar, eggs,
cinnamon, ginger and salt; process until well mixed. Pour into
ungreased 1-quart soufflé dish. Cover tightly with foil. Crumple large
sheet (about 15×12 inches) of foil; place on bottom of slow cooker.
Pour 2 cups water over foil. Make foil handles using technique on
page 10. Place soufflé dish on top of foil strips.

TRANSFER dish to slow cooker using foil handles; lay foil strips over
top of dish. Cover and cook on HIGH 2½ to 3 hours or until skewer
inserted in center comes out clean. Using foil strips, lift dish from
slow cooker and transfer to wire rack. Uncover; let stand 30 minutes.
Garnish with whipped cream and nutmeg, if desired.

Makes 4 servings

*Nutrients per Serving: Calories 372, Total Fat 9 g, Protein 11 g,
Carbohydrate 62 g, Cholesterol 131 mg, Sodium 351 mg, Dietary Fiber 2 g
Dietary Exchanges: ½ Milk, 3½ Bread, 2 Fat*

Fruit & Nut Baked Apples

4 large baking apples, such
as Rome Beauty or
Cortland
1 tablespoon lemon juice
⅓ cup chopped dried
apricots
⅓ cup chopped walnuts or
pecans

3 tablespoons packed
brown sugar
½ teaspoon ground
cinnamon
2 tablespoons melted
butter or margarine

SCOOP out center of each apple, leaving 1½-inch-wide cavity about
½ inch from bottom. Peel top of apple down about 1 inch. Brush
peeled edges evenly with lemon juice. Mix apricots, walnuts, brown
sugar and cinnamon in small bowl. Add butter; mix well. Spoon
mixture evenly into apple cavities.

POUR ½ cup water onto bottom of slow cooker. Place 2 apples in
slow cooker. Arrange remaining 2 apples above but not directly on
top of bottom apples. Cover and cook on LOW 3 to 4 hours or until
apples are tender. Serve warm or at room temperature with caramel
ice cream topping, if desired. *Makes 4 servings*

*Nutrients per Serving: Calories 260, Total Fat 12 g, Protein 3 g,
Carbohydrate 40 g, Cholesterol 15 mg, Sodium 64 mg, Dietary Fiber 4 g
Dietary Exchanges: 2½ Fruit, 2½ Fat*

*Ever wonder why you need to brush
lemon juice onto apples to keep them from
browning? Citrus fruits contain an acid that
keeps apples, potatoes and other white
vegetables from discoloring once they are cut
or peeled.*

Boston Brown Bread

3 (16-ounce) emptied and
    cleaned cans
½ cup rye flour
½ cup yellow cornmeal
½ cup whole wheat flour
3 tablespoons sugar

1 teaspoon baking soda
¾ teaspoon salt
½ cup chopped walnuts
½ cup raisins
1 cup buttermilk*
⅓ cup molasses

SPRAY cans and 1 side of three 6-inch-square pieces of aluminum foil with nonstick cooking spray; set aside. Combine rye flour, cornmeal, whole wheat flour, sugar, baking soda and salt in large bowl. Stir in walnuts and raisins. Whisk buttermilk and molasses in medium bowl until blended. Add buttermilk mixture to dry ingredients; stir until well mixed. Spoon mixture evenly into prepared cans. Place 1 piece of foil, greased side down, on top of each can. Secure foil with rubber bands or cotton string.

PLACE filled cans in slow cooker. Pour enough boiling water into slow cooker to come halfway up sides of cans. (Make sure foil tops do not touch boiling water.) Cover and cook on LOW 4 hours or until skewer inserted in centers comes out clean. To remove bread, lay cans on side; roll and tap gently on all sides until bread releases. Cool completely on wire racks. *Makes 3 loaves*

*Soured fresh milk may be substituted. To sour, place 1 tablespoon lemon juice plus enough milk to equal 1 cup in 2-cup measure. Stir; let stand 5 minutes before using.

Nutrients per Serving: Calories 93, Total Fat 2 g, Protein 2 g, Carbohydrate 17 g, Cholesterol <1 mg, Sodium 181 mg, Dietary Fiber 2 g Dietary Exchanges: 1 Bread, ½ Fat

Poached Pears with Raspberry Sauce

4 cups cran-raspberry juice cocktail

2 cups Rhine or Riesling wine

¼ cup sugar

2 cinnamon sticks, broken into halves

4 to 5 firm Bosc or Anjou pears, peeled, cored and seeded

1 package (10 ounces) frozen raspberries in syrup, thawed

Fresh berries (optional)

COMBINE juice, wine, sugar and cinnamon stick halves in slow cooker. Submerge pears in mixture. Cover and cook on LOW 3½ to 4 hours or until pears are tender. Remove and discard cinnamon sticks.

PROCESS raspberries in food processor or blender until smooth; strain out seeds. Spoon raspberry sauce onto serving plates; place pear on top of sauce. Garnish with fresh berries, if desired.

Makes 4 to 5 servings

Nutrients per Serving: Calories 429, Total Fat 1 g, Protein 1 g, Carbohydrate 90 g, Cholesterol 0 mg, Sodium 18 mg, Dietary Fiber 7 g
Dietary Exchanges: 6 Fruit, 1½ Fat*

*Fat exchange accounts for the calories from the alcohol.

Vary the look of this dessert by leaving some peel on the pears. To make stripes, peel off a curved strip using a vegetable peeler or paring knife, then leave the next strip of peel on the pear. Continue until you've gone all the way around the pear. After poaching, the remaining strips of peel can be removed from the pear to reveal the white flesh. The sections that were peeled before poaching will be pink.

English Bread Pudding

16 slices day-old, firm-
    textured white bread
    (1 small loaf)
1¾ cups milk
  1 package (8 ounces)
    mixed dried fruit, cut
    into small pieces
½ cup chopped nuts
  1 medium apple, cored and
    chopped

¼ cup butter or margarine,
    melted
⅓ cup packed brown sugar
  1 egg, lightly beaten
  1 teaspoon ground
    cinnamon
¼ teaspoon ground nutmeg
¼ teaspoon ground cloves

TEAR bread, with crusts, into 1- to 2-inch pieces. Place in slow cooker. Pour milk over bread; let soak 30 minutes. Stir in dried fruit, nuts and apple. Combine remaining ingredients in small bowl. Pour over bread mixture. Stir well to blend. Cover and cook on LOW 3½ to 4 hours or until skewer inserted in center comes out clean.

Makes 6 to 8 servings

Nutrients per Serving: Calories 516, Total Fat 19 g, Protein 12 g, Carbohydrate 80 g, Cholesterol 61 mg, Sodium 446 mg, Dietary Fiber 5 g
Dietary Exchanges: 3 Fruit, 2 Bread, 1 Meat, 3 Fat

Cook's Nook

Chopping dried fruits can be difficult. To make the job easier, cut the fruit with kitchen scissors. You can also spray your scissors or chef's knife with nonstick cooking spray before you begin chopping so that the fruit won't stick to the blade.

Spiced Apple & Cranberry Compote

1 package (6 ounces) dried
    apples
½ cup (2 ounces) dried
    cranberries
2½ cups cranberry juice
    cocktail
½ cup Rhine wine or apple
    juice

½ cup honey
2 cinnamon sticks, broken
    into halves
Frozen yogurt or ice
    cream (optional)
Additional cinnamon
    sticks (optional)

MIX apples, cranberries, juice, wine, honey and cinnamon stick halves in slow cooker. Cover and cook on LOW 4 to 5 hours or until liquid is absorbed and fruit is tender. Remove and discard cinnamon stick halves. Ladle compote into bowls. Serve warm, at room temperature or chilled with scoop of frozen yogurt. Garnish with additional cinnamon sticks, if desired.   *Makes 6 servings*

Nutrients per Serving: Calories 238, Total Fat <1 g, Protein <1 g, Carbohydrate 59 g, Cholesterol 0 mg, Sodium 31 mg, Dietary Fiber 4 g Dietary Exchanges: 4 Fruit

FAST & EASY STIR-FRIES

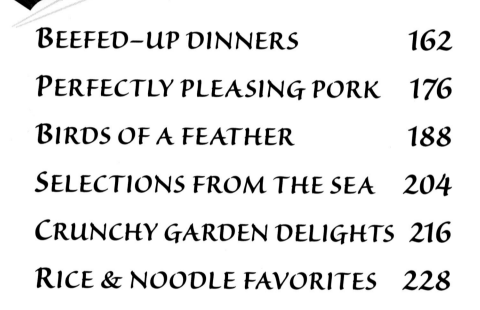

BEEFED-UP DINNERS

BEEF WITH CASHEWS

1 piece fresh ginger (about 1 inch square)

1 pound beef rump steak, trimmed

4 tablespoons vegetable oil, divided

4 teaspoons cornstarch

½ cup water

4 teaspoons soy sauce

1 teaspoon sesame oil

1 teaspoon oyster sauce

1 teaspoon Chinese chili sauce

8 green onions with tops, cut into 1-inch pieces

2 cloves garlic, minced

⅔ cup unsalted roasted cashews (about 3 ounces)

1. Peel and finely chop ginger; set aside. Cut meat across grain into thin slices about 2 inches long.

2. Heat 1 tablespoon vegetable oil in wok over high heat. Add ½ of meat; stir-fry until browned, 3 to 5 minutes. Remove from wok; set aside. Repeat with 1 tablespoon oil and remaining meat.

3. Combine cornstarch, water, soy sauce, sesame oil, oyster sauce and chili sauce in small bowl; mix well.

4. Heat remaining 2 tablespoons vegetable oil in wok or large skillet over high heat. Add ginger, onions, garlic and cashews; stir-fry 1 minute. Stir cornstarch mixture; add to wok with meat. Cook and stir until liquid boils and thickens. *Makes 4 servings*

Beef with Cashews

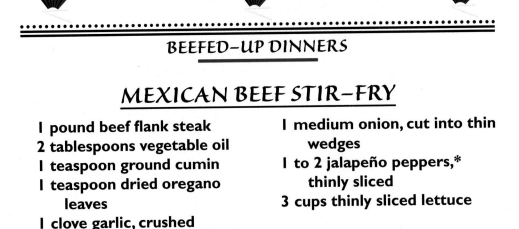
MEXICAN BEEF STIR–FRY

1 pound beef flank steak
2 tablespoons vegetable oil
1 teaspoon ground cumin
1 teaspoon dried oregano
 leaves
1 clove garlic, crushed
1 red or green bell pepper,
 cut into thin strips

1 medium onion, cut into thin
 wedges
1 to 2 jalapeño peppers,*
 thinly sliced
3 cups thinly sliced lettuce

*Remove interior ribs and seeds if a milder flavor is desired.

Cut beef steak into ⅛-inch-thick strips. Combine oil, cumin, oregano and garlic in small bowl. Heat ½ oil mixture in large nonstick skillet over medium-high heat. Add bell pepper, onion and jalapeño pepper; stir-fry 2 to 3 minutes or until crisp-tender. Remove and reserve. In same skillet, stir-fry beef strips (½ at a time) in remaining oil mixture 1 to 2 minutes. Return vegetables to skillet and heat through. Serve beef mixture over lettuce. *Makes 4 servings*

 Tip: Recipe may also be prepared using beef top sirloin or top round steak cut 1 inch thick.

 Serving Suggestion: Serve with corn bread twists.

Favorite recipe from **North Dakota Beef Commission**

TANGY PLUM SHORT RIBS

2 tablespoons vegetable oil
1 teaspoon chopped garlic
¾ pound cooked short ribs,
 cut into small pieces

3 tablespoons LEE KUM
 KEE® Plum Sauce
1 tablespoon LEE KUM KEE®
 Oyster Flavored Sauce

Heat skillet over medium heat. Add oil. Sauté garlic. Add short ribs and stir-fry until heated through. Add Plum Sauce and Oyster Flavored Sauce. Stir well and serve. *Makes 4 servings*

Mexican Beef Stir-Fry

BEEF AND GRAVY STIR–FRY

8 ounces uncooked egg
noodles

1 tablespoon extra-virgin
olive oil, divided

1½ pounds beef sirloin, cut into
thin strips

2 cloves garlic, minced

⅓ cup all-purpose flour

1 tablespoon beef bouillon
granules

2 tablespoons dry red wine

½ teaspoon dried thyme
leaves

¾ teaspoon sugar

½ teaspoon salt

¼ teaspoon black pepper

3 tablespoons chopped
parsley

1. Cook noodles according to package directions.

2. Meanwhile, place 1½ teaspoons oil in large nonstick skillet or wok. Heat skillet over medium-high heat 1 minute. Add half of beef and cook, stirring, 3 minutes. Place on plate with any accumulated juices and set aside. Add remaining 1½ teaspoons oil to skillet; add remaining beef and garlic; repeat cooking process. Place on plate with reserved beef and juices.

3. Add flour to skillet; cook and stir 6 to 7 minutes or until aromatic and flour begins to turn golden. Remove from heat; cool slightly by stirring 1 additional minute. Slowly whisk in ½ cup water to make a paste. Slowly whisk in 1½ cups additional water (mixture may be lumpy). Stir in bouillon granules, wine, thyme, sugar, salt and pepper along with reserved beef and any accumulated juices. Return mixture to a boil over medium-high heat. Cook 8 to 10 minutes or until slightly thickened.

4. Place noodles on serving platter. Spoon beef mixture over noodles and top with parsley. *Makes 4 servings*

Beef and Gravy Stir-Fry

FIVE-SPICE BEEF STIR-FRY

1 pound beef top sirloin, cut into thin strips

2 tablespoons light soy sauce

2 tablespoons plus 1½ teaspoons cornstarch, divided

3 tablespoons walnut or vegetable oil, divided

4 medium carrots, cut into matchstick-size pieces (about 2 cups)

1 red bell pepper, cut into chunks

1 yellow bell pepper, cut into chunks

1 cup chopped onion

¼ to ½ teaspoon red pepper flakes

1 tablespoon plus 1½ teaspoons packed dark brown sugar

2 teaspoons beef bouillon granules

1 teaspoon Chinese five-spice powder

3 cups hot cooked rice

½ cup honey roasted peanuts

1. Place beef in shallow glass baking dish. Combine soy sauce and 2 tablespoons cornstarch in small bowl. Pour soy sauce mixture over beef; toss to coat thoroughly. Set aside.

2. Meanwhile, add 1 tablespoon oil to large nonstick skillet or wok. Heat skillet over high heat 1 minute or until hot. Add carrots. Cook and stir 3 to 4 minutes or until edges begin to brown. Remove carrots and set aside. Reduce heat to medium-high. Add 1 tablespoon oil, bell peppers, onion and red pepper; cook and stir 4 minutes or until onion is translucent. Remove vegetables and set aside separately from carrots.

3. Add remaining 1 tablespoon oil to skillet. Add beef; cook and stir 6 minutes.

4. Meanwhile, in small bowl, combine 1½ cups water with brown sugar, bouillon granules, five-spice powder and remaining 1½ teaspoons cornstarch. Stir until cornstarch is completely dissolved. Increase heat to high. Add bouillon mixture and reserved bell peppers and onion to skillet; bring to a boil. Cook and stir 2 to 3 minutes or until slightly thickened.

5. Toss rice with carrots; place on serving platter. Spoon beef mixture over rice and sprinkle peanuts over beef mixture.

Makes 4 servings

BEEFY GREEN BEAN & WALNUT STIR-FRY

1 teaspoon vegetable oil	1 teaspoon salt
3 cloves garlic, minced	½ cup California walnut
1 pound lean ground beef or	pieces
ground turkey	Hot cooked egg noodles or
1 bag (16 ounces) **BIRDS**	rice (optional)
EYE® frozen Cut Green	
Beans, thawed	

• In large skillet, heat oil and garlic over medium heat about 30 seconds.

• Add beef and beans; sprinkle with salt. Mix well.

• Cook 5 minutes or until beef is well browned, stirring occasionally.

• Stir in walnuts; cook 2 minutes more.

• Serve over noodles, if desired.   *Makes 4 servings*

Prep Time: 5 minutes
Cook Time: 7 to 10 minutes

SATAY BEEF

1 pound beef tenderloin,
   trimmed
1 teaspoon cornstarch
5 tablespoons water, divided
3½ teaspoons soy sauce,
   divided
1 to 2 teaspoons sesame oil
2 tablespoons vegetable oil
1 medium yellow onion,
   coarsely chopped

1 clove garlic, minced
1 tablespoon dry sherry
1 tablespoon satay sauce
1 teaspoon curry powder
½ teaspoon sugar
   Fresh chervil and carrot
    flowers* for garnish

*To make carrot garnish, cut carrot crosswise into thin slices; cut into desired shape with small decorative cutter or sharp knife.

1. Cut meat across grain into thin slices; flatten each slice by pressing with fingers.

2. Combine cornstarch, 3 tablespoons water, 1½ teaspoons soy sauce and sesame oil; mix well. Add to meat in medium bowl; stir to coat well. Let stand 20 minutes.

3. Heat vegetable oil in wok or large skillet over high heat. Add ½ of meat, spreading out slices so they do not overlap.

4. Cook meat slices on each side just until lightly browned, 2 to 3 minutes. Remove from wok; set aside. Repeat with remaining meat slices.

5. Add onion and garlic to wok; stir-fry until tender, about 3 minutes.

6. Combine remaining 2 tablespoons water, 2 teaspoons soy sauce, sherry, satay sauce, curry powder and sugar in small cup. Add to wok; cook and stir until liquid boils. Return meat to wok; cook and stir until thoroughly heated. Garnish, if desired.   *Makes 4 servings*

Satay Beef

HOT GLAZED BEEF ON SAFFRON-ONION RICE

1½ pounds beef sirloin, cut into thin strips
¼ cup bourbon
½ cup packed dark brown sugar
½ cup light soy sauce
½ teaspoon red pepper flakes
1 large package yellow saffron rice

2 tablespoons vegetable oil, divided
2 cups chopped onions
1 cup chopped red bell pepper
1 can (8 ounces) sliced water chestnuts, drained

1. Place beef in shallow glass baking dish.

2. Combine bourbon, brown sugar, soy sauce and red pepper flakes in small bowl; whisk until sugar has dissolved completely. Pour over beef and marinate 15 minutes, stirring occasionally.

3. Cook rice according to package directions.

4. Meanwhile, add 1 tablespoon oil to large nonstick skillet or wok. Heat over medium-high heat 1 minute. Add onions; cook 15 minutes or until richly browned. Remove from skillet and set aside.

5. Add remaining 1 tablespoon oil and bell pepper to skillet; cook 3 minutes.

6. Toss cooked rice with bell pepper, water chestnuts and onions. Place on serving platter; keep warm.

7. Drain beef; reserve marinade. Increase heat to high; add half of beef to skillet. Cook and stir 4 minutes or just until all liquid has evaporated. Place beef on top of rice mixture and keep warm. Add remaining beef; repeat cooking procedure and place on serving platter.

8. Reduce heat to medium-high. Add reserved marinade, scraping bottom and sides of skillet. Cook 4 minutes or until liquid is reduced to ⅓ cup. Drizzle cooked marinade over beef and serve immediately.

Makes 4 servings

Hot Glazed Beef on Saffron-Onion Rice

TERIYAKI CHOP SUEY

SAUCE

⅓ cup beef broth
3 tablespoons **LA CHOY**® Teriyaki Marinade & Sauce
1½ tablespoons cornstarch

1½ tablespoons packed brown sugar
1 teaspoon garlic powder
¼ teaspoon black pepper

BEEF AND VEGETABLES

1 tablespoon **LA CHOY**® Teriyaki Marinade & Sauce
1 tablespoon cornstarch
1 pound flank or sirloin steak, sliced across grain into thin 2-inch strips
3 tablespoons **WESSON**® Oil
2 cups sliced fresh mushrooms

1 (14-ounce) can **LA CHOY**® Bean Sprouts, drained
1 (14-ounce) can **LA CHOY**® Chop Suey Vegetables, drained
½ cup diagonally cut ½-inch green onion pieces
1 (5-ounce) can **LA CHOY**® Chow Mein Noodles

In small bowl, combine sauce ingredients; set aside. In medium bowl, combine teriyaki sauce and cornstarch. Add beef; toss gently. In large nonstick skillet or wok, heat oil. Add half of beef mixture; stir-fry until lightly browned. Remove beef from skillet; set aside. Repeat with remaining beef mixture. Add mushrooms to skillet; stir-fry 1 minute. Add bean sprouts and chop suey vegetables; heat thoroughly, stirring occasionally. Stir sauce; add to skillet with beef and green onions. Cook, stirring constantly, until sauce is thick and bubbly. Garnish, if desired. Serve over noodles.   *Makes 4 to 6 servings*

THAI BEEF & PEANUTS

1 pound beef full cut round
   steak, cut into
   2×½×¼-inch strips
2 tablespoons vegetable oil,
   divided
¼ to ½ teaspoon red pepper
   flakes
2 medium onions, cut into
   half-rings
2 red bell peppers, cut into
   ¼-inch strips

2 medium yellow squash
   (about 4 ounces),
   julienned (slice on the
   diagonal, then cut each
   slice into ¼-inch-wide
   strips)
½ cup Thai peanut sauce*
¼ cup dry roasted peanuts,
   coarsely chopped

Available in larger grocery stores or specialty markets.

1. In large skillet, heat 1 tablespoon oil over medium-high heat until hot. Add beef strips. Cook, stirring frequently, about 4 minutes or until outside surface is no longer pink. Remove beef from skillet.

2. Add remaining 1 tablespoon oil to skillet. Add red pepper flakes and onions, stirring constantly about 3 minutes or until onions begin to soften.

3. Add bell peppers, stirring constantly about 3 minutes or until bell peppers begin to soften.

4. Add squash; cook about 1 minute.

5. Add peanut sauce and return beef to skillet; cook about 3 to 5 minutes or until heated through.

6. Sprinkle peanuts over beef mixture. Serve over cooked couscous or rice.

Makes 4 servings

Favorite recipe from **North Dakota Beef Commission**

PERFECTLY PLEASING PORK

HONEY NUT STIR-FRY

1 pound pork steak or loin or
   boneless chicken breast
¾ cup orange juice
⅓ cup honey
3 tablespoons soy sauce
1 tablespoon cornstarch
¼ teaspoon ground ginger
2 tablespoons vegetable oil,
   divided

2 large carrots, sliced
   diagonally
2 stalks celery, sliced
   diagonally
½ cup cashews or peanuts
   Hot cooked rice

Cut pork into thin strips; set aside. Combine orange juice, honey, soy sauce, cornstarch and ginger in small bowl; mix well. Heat 1 tablespoon oil in large skillet over medium-high heat. Add carrots and celery; stir-fry about 3 minutes. Remove vegetables; set aside. Pour remaining 1 tablespoon oil into skillet. Add pork; stir-fry about 3 minutes. Return vegetables to skillet; add honey mixture and nuts. Cook and stir over medium-high heat until sauce comes to a boil and thickens. Serve over rice. *Makes 4 to 6 servings*

Favorite recipe from **National Honey Board**

Honey Nut Stir-Fry

SWEET AND SOUR PORK

¾ pound boneless pork
1 teaspoon vegetable oil
1 bag (16 ounces) **BIRDS EYE®** frozen Farm Fresh Mixtures Pepper Stir Fry vegetables

1 tablespoon water
1 jar (14 ounces) sweet and sour sauce
1 can (8 ounces) pineapple chunks, drained
Hot cooked rice (optional)

• Cut pork into thin strips.

• In large skillet, heat oil over medium-high heat.

• Add pork; stir-fry until pork is browned.

• Add vegetables and water; cover and cook over medium heat 5 to 7 minutes or until vegetables are crisp-tender.

• Uncover; stir in sweet and sour sauce and pineapple. Cook until heated through. Serve over rice, if desired.   *Makes 4 servings*

SPAM™ HOT & SPICY STIR–FRY

⅓ cup reduced-sodium teriyaki sauce
⅓ cup water
2 to 3 teaspoons **HOUSE OF TSANG®** Chinese Hot Oil
½ teaspoon ground ginger
1 (12-ounce) can **SPAM®** Lite Luncheon Meat, cubed
1 cup broccoli florets
1 cup chopped onion

1 cup snow peas
1 red bell pepper, cut into strips
1 tablespoon plus 1½ teaspoons vegetable oil
1 (14-ounce) can whole baby corn, drained, halved
1 (7-ounce) jar mushrooms, drained
6 cups hot cooked white rice

In small bowl, combine teriyaki sauce, water, Chinese hot oil and ginger; set aside. In wok or large skillet, stir-fry SPAM®, broccoli, onion, snow peas and bell pepper in vegetable oil 2 minutes. Add teriyaki sauce mixture; cook until bubbly. Add baby corn and mushrooms; heat thoroughly. Serve over rice.   *Makes 6 servings*

Sweet and Sour Pork

STIR–FRIED PORK WITH ORANGES AND SNOW PEAS

I cup uncooked rice

I tablespoon vegetable oil

I pound lean boneless pork, cut into ¼-inch strips

½ pound snow peas, trimmed

½ cup bottled stir-fry sauce

2 tablespoons thawed frozen orange juice concentrate

I can (11 ounces) mandarin orange sections, drained

Cook rice according to package directions. Heat oil in wok or large skillet over high heat until hot. Stir-fry pork 3 minutes or until brown. Add snow peas; stir-fry 2 minutes or until crisp-tender. Add sauce and juice concentrate; stir until well blended. Gently stir in orange sections; heat through. Serve with rice.   *Makes 4 servings*

PLUM–GOOD PORK

I pound boneless pork loin, cut into thin stir-fry strips

2 teaspoons vegetable oil, divided

I tablespoon grated ginger

½ red bell pepper, cut into 1-inch squares

½ green bell pepper, cut into 1-inch squares

I cup mushrooms, sliced

6 fresh plums, seeded and cut into halves

I cup peach nectar

⅓ cup lime juice

I tablespoon cornstarch

2 tablespoons soy sauce

¼ teaspoon ground cinnamon

½ teaspoon dry mustard

I teaspoon grated fresh orange peel

Heat I teaspoon oil over high heat in nonstick skillet; stir-fry pork strips with ginger about 3 minutes. Remove from skillet. Heat remaining I teaspoon oil in skillet; stir-fry peppers and mushrooms 3 minutes. Add plums and stir-fry 2 minutes. Combine remaining ingredients well; add to skillet with pork. Cook and stir until sauce bubbles and thickens.   *Makes 4 servings*

Favorite recipe from **National Pork Producers Council**

Stir-Fried Pork with Oranges and Snow Peas

STIR–FRIED PORK WITH GREEN BEANS AND BABY CORN

¾ pound pork tenderloin

4 teaspoons cornstarch, divided

2 tablespoons soy sauce

1 tablespoon rice wine or dry sherry

1 teaspoon sugar

½ teaspoon sesame oil

⅓ cup plus 2 tablespoons water, divided

1 pound fresh green beans

2 tablespoons peanut oil, divided

2 cloves garlic, minced

1 teaspoon finely chopped fresh ginger

1 tablespoon black bean sauce

1 can (14 ounces) pre-cut baby corn, drained and rinsed or 1 can (15 ounces) whole baby corn, drained, rinsed and cut into 1-inch lengths

1. Slice pork across the grain into thin slices; cut into ¾-inch strips.

2. Combine 1 teaspoon cornstarch, soy sauce, rice wine, sugar and sesame oil in medium bowl; mix well. Add pork; toss to coat. Set aside to marinate 20 to 30 minutes. Combine remaining 3 teaspoons cornstarch and ⅓ cup water in small cup; set aside.

3. To prepare beans, snap off stem ends from beans, pulling strings down to remove if necessary. Cut beans diagonally into 1½-inch lengths.

4. Heat 1 tablespoon peanut oil in wok or large skillet over high heat. Add beans; stir-fry about 4 minutes. Add remaining 2 tablespoons water; reduce heat to medium-low. Cover and simmer 10 to 12 minutes or until crisp-tender. Remove beans from wok; set aside.

5. Heat remaining 1 tablespoon peanut oil in wok over high heat. Add garlic, ginger and pork; stir-fry about 3 minutes or until meat is no longer pink in center. Add black bean sauce; stir-fry 1 minute.

6. Return beans to wok. Stir cornstarch mixture; add to wok. Bring to a boil; cook until sauce thickens. Stir in baby corn; heat through.

Makes 4 servings

Stir-Fried Pork with Green Beans and Baby Corn

SPICY TOMATO–PORK STIR–FRY

2 cups uncooked instant rice
⅔ cup tomato juice
1 tablespoon cornstarch
2 tablespoons soy sauce
¼ teaspoon paprika
3 boneless pork chops
¼ teaspoon garlic salt

⅛ teaspoon red pepper flakes
2 slices uncooked bacon, chopped
3 medium tomatoes, chopped
2 green onions with tops, sliced diagonally

Prepare rice; set aside. Combine juice, cornstarch, soy sauce and paprika, stirring until cornstarch dissolves. Set aside. Slice pork across grain into ¼-inch slices; place in medium bowl. Sprinkle with garlic salt and pepper flakes. Cook bacon. Remove using slotted spoon; set aside. Add pork, tomatoes and onions to skillet; cook 3 minutes or until pork is barely pink in center. Stir in tomato juice mixture; cook, stirring constantly, until sauce thickens slightly. Stir in bacon and serve over rice. *Makes 4 servings*

CHINESE PORK & VEGETABLE STIR–FRY

2 tablespoons vegetable oil, divided
1 pound pork tenderloin, cut into ¼-inch slices
6 cups assorted fresh vegetables*
1 can (8 ounces) sliced water chestnuts, drained

1 envelope LIPTON® Recipe Secrets® Onion Soup Mix
¾ cup water
½ cup orange juice
1 tablespoon soy sauce
¼ teaspoon garlic powder

Broccoli florets, snow peas, thinly sliced red or green bell peppers or carrots can be used.

In 12-inch skillet, heat 1 tablespoon oil over medium-high heat; brown pork. Remove and set aside. In same skillet, heat remaining 1 tablespoon oil and cook vegetables, stirring occasionally, 5 minutes. Stir in remaining ingredients. Bring to a boil. Reduce heat to low; simmer, uncovered, 3 minutes. Add pork to skillet; cook 1 minute or until heated through. *Makes about 4 servings*

Spicy Tomato-Pork Stir-Fry

PORK TENDERLOIN WITH MANDARIN SALSA

1½ pounds boneless pork loin chops, cut into ¼-inch strips

1 cup orange juice

1 medium green bell pepper, finely chopped

1 can (10½ ounces) mandarin orange segments, drained and chopped

1⅓ cups chopped red onion, divided

½ cup frozen whole kernel corn, thawed

2 tablespoons olive oil, divided

4 teaspoons bottled minced garlic, divided

1½ teaspoons chili powder, divided

1¼ teaspoons salt, divided

1½ teaspoons cumin

¼ teaspoon ground black pepper

1. Combine pork and orange juice in medium bowl. Set aside.

2. To prepare Mandarin Salsa, combine bell pepper, mandarin oranges, ⅓ cup onion, corn, 1 tablespoon oil, 1 teaspoon garlic, ¼ teaspoon chili powder and ¼ teaspoon salt in another medium bowl. Set aside.

3. Heat remaining 1 tablespoon oil in large nonstick skillet over medium-high heat. Add remaining 1 cup onion and 3 teaspoons garlic. Cook and stir 5 minutes or until onion is softened and starting to brown.

4. Meanwhile, drain pork, reserving orange juice marinade. Toss pork, remaining 1¼ teaspoons chili powder, cumin, remaining 1 teaspoon salt and black pepper in large bowl; add to skillet. Cook and stir 5 minutes or until pork is cooked through and lightly browned. Add ⅓ cup reserved orange juice marinade to skillet; bring to a boil. Reduce heat; simmer 1 to 2 minutes or until liquid thickens slightly. Serve immediately with Mandarin Salsa.   *Makes 4 servings*

Prep and Cook Time: 21 minutes

Pork Tenderloin with Mandarin Salsa

BIRDS OF A FEATHER

CHICKEN STIR–FRY

**4 boneless skinless chicken
   breast halves (about 1½
   pounds)
2 tablespoons vegetable oil
1 tablespoon cornstarch
2 tablespoons light soy sauce
2 tablespoons orange juice**

**1 bag (16 ounces) BIRDS
   EYE® frozen Farm Fresh
   Mixtures Broccoli,
   Carrots & Water
   Chestnuts
Hot cooked rice (optional)**

• Cut chicken into ½-inch-thick long strips.

• In wok or large skillet, heat oil over medium-high heat.

• Add chicken; cook 5 minutes, stirring occasionally.

• Meanwhile, in small bowl, combine cornstarch, soy sauce and
orange juice; blend well and set aside.

• Add vegetables to chicken; cook 5 minutes more or until chicken is
no longer pink in center, stirring occasionally.

• Stir in soy sauce mixture; cook 1 minute or until heated through.

• Serve over rice, if desired.   *Makes 4 servings*

Prep Time: 5 minutes
Cook Time: 12 minutes

Chicken Stir-Fry

ITALIAN–STYLE CHICKEN STIR–FRY

1 tablespoon olive oil
1 pound boneless skinless
   chicken breast meat, cut
   into thin strips
1 cup (1 small) thinly sliced
   green bell pepper
1 cup (1 small) thinly sliced
   onion

2 cups (1-pound-1-ounce can)
   CONTADINA® Dalla
   Casa Buitoni Country
   Italian Cooking Sauce,
   Cacciatore
½ cup (2¼-ounce can) sliced
   ripe olives, drained
3 to 4 pita breads, warmed

HEAT oil in large skillet over high heat. Add chicken, bell pepper and onion; cook, stirring constantly, 5 to 6 minutes or until chicken is no longer pink in center. Add cooking sauce and olives; heat through.

CUT pitas in half; stuff mixture into pockets.

Makes 3 to 4 servings

KUNG PAO CHICKEN

1 pound boneless skinless
   chicken breasts, cut into
   1-inch pieces
1 tablespoon cornstarch
2 teaspoons **CRISCO**®
   Vegetable Oil
3 tablespoons chopped green
   onions with tops
2 cloves garlic, minced
¼ to 1½ teaspoons red
   pepper flakes

¼ to ½ teaspoon ground
   ginger
2 tablespoons wine vinegar
2 tablespoons soy sauce
2 teaspoons sugar
⅓ cup unsalted dry roasted
   peanuts
4 cups hot cooked rice
   (cooked without salt or
   fat)

1. Combine chicken and cornstarch in small bowl; toss. Heat Crisco® Oil in large skillet or wok on medium-high heat. Add chicken. Stir-fry 5 to 7 minutes or until no longer pink in center. Remove from skillet. Add onions, garlic, pepper and ginger to skillet. Stir-fry 15 seconds. Remove from heat.

2. Combine vinegar, soy sauce and sugar in small bowl. Stir well. Add to skillet. Return chicken to skillet. Stir until coated. Stir in nuts. Heat thoroughly, stirring occasionally. Serve over hot rice.

Makes 4 servings

TERIYAKI STIR-FRY CHICKEN DINNER

1 package (about 1¾ pounds) **PERDUE**® **Fresh Chicken or Oven Stuffer**® **Wingettes (12 to 16)**
Salt to taste
Ground black pepper to taste
2 tablespoons vegetable oil
1 bunch broccoli, florets only (1 cup)
1 can (8 ounces) sliced water chestnuts, drained
4 carrots, sliced
4 green onions, thinly sliced
½ cup water
¼ cup soy sauce
¼ cup packed brown sugar
3 tablespoons dry sherry or white vinegar
2 cloves garlic, finely chopped
2 teaspoons grated fresh ginger
2 cups warm cooked rice
Additional sliced green onions for garnish (optional)

Sprinkle wingettes with salt and pepper.

In large nonstick wok or skillet over medium-high heat, heat oil. Stir-fry broccoli 1 minute; add water chestnuts and carrots. Stir-fry 1 minute longer and add onions; stir-fry a few seconds. Remove vegetables and reserve.

Add wingettes to wok and cook until lightly browned on all sides, about 5 minutes. Reduce heat to low; cover and cook 10 minutes, turning occasionally. Remove wingettes to paper towel and pour off drippings. Return wingettes and vegetables to wok. Add remaining ingredients except rice and green onions; stir until well mixed. Cook, turning frequently, until wingettes are glazed and sauce is thickened, about 3 to 5 minutes. Serve hot over rice, sprinkling with additional green onions, if desired.

Makes 4 to 6 servings

LEMON CHICKEN WITH WALNUTS

¼ cup **FILIPPO BERIO®** Olive
    Oil, divided
½ cup chopped walnuts
4 boneless skinless chicken
    breast halves, pounded
    thin
2 tablespoons all-purpose
    flour
1 medium onion, chopped
1 clove garlic, minced

1 cup dry white wine
2 carrots, very thinly sliced
¼ cup lemon juice
½ teaspoon dried thyme
    leaves
1 zucchini, very thinly sliced
1 yellow squash, very thinly
    sliced
Chopped fresh parsley

In large skillet, heat 2 tablespoons olive oil over medium-high heat until hot. Add walnuts; cook and stir 2 to 3 minutes or until lightly browned. Remove with slotted spoon; reserve. Lightly coat chicken breasts in flour. Add remaining 2 tablespoons olive oil to skillet; heat over medium-high heat until hot. Add chicken, onion and garlic; cook 5 minutes or until chicken is brown, turning chicken and stirring occasionally. Add wine, carrots, lemon juice and thyme. Cover; reduce heat to low and simmer 8 minutes. Add zucchini and squash; cover and simmer 2 minutes or until vegetables are crisp-tender and chicken is no longer pink in center. Remove chicken and vegetables; keep warm. Boil sauce until slightly thickened. Pour over chicken and vegetables. Top with reserved walnuts and parsley.

Makes 4 servings

STIR–FRIED CHICKEN WITH BLACK PEPPER SAUCE

½ cup **LEE KUM KEE®** Black
    Pepper Sauce, divided
2 teaspoons cornstarch
¾ pound boneless chicken, cut
    into bite-size pieces
2 tablespoons vegetable oil

¼ pound onion, cut into bite-
    size pieces
2 ounces red bell pepper, cut
    into bite-size pieces
¼ pound pineapple chunks

continued on page 194

Lemon Chicken with Walnuts

Stir-Fried Chicken with Black Pepper Sauce, continued

1. Combine ¼ cup Black Pepper Sauce and cornstarch in large bowl; add chicken. Marinate chicken 5 minutes.

2. Heat oil in wok over high heat. Add onion and cook until fragrant. Add chicken and stir-fry 2 minutes.

3. Add bell pepper, pineapple and remaining ¼ cup Black Pepper Sauce; cook until heated through. *Makes 4 to 6 servings*

THAI DUCK WITH BEANS AND SPROUTS

¼ **cup teriyaki sauce, divided**	**1 cup chicken broth**
2 tablespoons vegetable oil,	**1 tablespoon cornstarch**
divided	½ **teaspoon ground ginger**
1 tablespoon white wine	**3 cups fresh green beans,**
vinegar	**stemmed and cut into**
1 clove garlic, minced	**halves**
1 pound boneless skinless	**1½ cups bean sprouts**
duck breast, cut into	**4 green onions with tops, cut**
¼-**inch strips**	**into 1-inch pieces**

1. Combine 2 tablespoons teriyaki sauce, 1 tablespoon oil, vinegar and garlic in medium bowl. Add duck; toss to coat well. Cover and refrigerate 45 minutes to 8 hours.

2. Whisk together chicken broth, cornstarch and ginger in small bowl; set aside.

3. Heat remaining 1 tablespoon oil in wok or large skillet over high heat. Drain duck, discarding marinade. Add duck to wok; stir-fry 4 minutes or until no longer pink. Remove duck from wok with slotted spoon.

4. Add green beans to liquid in wok; stir-fry 5 to 6 minutes or until crisp-tender. Add bean sprouts and onions. Stir-fry 2 minutes or until all vegetables are crisp-tender. Add chicken broth mixture and duck; stir until sauce thickens. *Makes 4 servings*

Thai Duck with Beans and Sprouts

MANDARIN CASHEW CHICKEN

SAUCE

½ cup syrup, reserved from mandarin oranges (see below)

¼ cup chicken broth

2 tablespoons sugar

1½ tablespoons **LA CHOY®** Soy Sauce

1½ tablespoons cornstarch

1 teaspoon rice vinegar

CHICKEN AND VEGETABLES

1 tablespoon **LA CHOY®** Soy Sauce

1 tablespoon cornstarch

1½ pounds boneless skinless chicken breasts, cut into thin 2-inch strips

4 tablespoons **WESSON®** Oil, divided

2 cups fresh broccoli florets

1 teaspoon minced fresh garlic

1 teaspoon minced fresh ginger

1 (8-ounce) can **LA CHOY®** Sliced Water Chestnuts, drained

4 green onions, diagonally sliced

1 (11-ounce) can mandarin orange slices, syrup drained and reserved for sauce

1 cup roasted cashews

In small bowl, combine sauce ingredients; set aside. In medium bowl, combine soy sauce and cornstarch; mix well. Add chicken; toss gently to coat. In large nonstick skillet or wok, heat 3 tablespoons oil. Add half of chicken mixture; stir-fry until chicken is no longer pink in center. Remove chicken from skillet; set aside. Repeat with remaining chicken mixture. Heat remaining 1 tablespoon oil in same skillet. Add broccoli, garlic and ginger; stir-fry 2 minutes. Stir sauce; add to skillet with water chestnuts and green onions. Cook, stirring constantly, until sauce is thick and bubbly. Return chicken to skillet with orange slices and cashews; heat thoroughly, stirring occasionally.

Makes 6 servings

MEXICAN CHICKEN STIR-FRY

1 package (about 1 pound)
  PERDUE® FIT 'N EASY®
  Fresh Skinless & Boneless
  Chicken Breast
  Tenderloins
1 teaspoon chili powder
½ teaspoon ground cumin
¼ teaspoon dried oregano
  leaves

2 tablespoons olive oil,
  divided
2 green onions, chopped
1 clove garlic, minced
1 can (4 ounces) chopped
  mild green chilies
1 can (19 ounces) black
  beans, rinsed and drained
Hot cooked rice

In medium bowl, place tenders. Add chili powder, cumin, oregano and 1 tablespoon oil; toss well. Heat wok or large nonstick skillet over medium-high heat. When hot, coat with remaining 1 tablespoon oil. Add tenders; stir-fry 4 to 5 minutes or until barely cooked through. Add onions, garlic, chilies and beans. Stir-fry 2 to 3 minutes or until heated through. Serve with rice.   *Makes 4 servings*

FESTIVE SWEET & SOUR STIR-FRY

2 cans (8 ounces each)
  pineapple chunks or
  crushed pineapple,
  undrained
2 medium carrots, sliced
1 medium green or red bell
  pepper, cut into chunks
1 medium onion, cut into
  chunks
2 tablespoons **WESSON®**
  Vegetable Oil

1 pound boneless skinless
  chicken breasts, cut into
  1-inch pieces
2 jars (10 ounces each)
  LA CHOY® Sweet & Sour
  Sauce
½ cup **LA CHOY®** Sliced
  Water Chestnuts
2 tablespoons **LA CHOY®** Soy
  Sauce
Hot cooked rice

Drain pineapple; reserve 2 tablespoons juice. Cook carrots, pepper and onion in hot oil in skillet until crisp-tender. Remove vegetables from skillet. Cook chicken in same skillet until browned. Add vegetables back to skillet with sweet and sour sauce, water chestnuts, soy sauce, pineapple and reserved juice. Heat through. Serve with rice.   *Makes 4 servings*

CHICKEN WITH LIME SAUCE

4 boneless skinless chicken
    breast halves
3 tablespoons lime juice
1 tablespoon plus 2
    teaspoons seasoned stir-
    fry or hot oil, divided
1 teaspoon grated lime peel
1 clove garlic, minced
½ teaspoon salt

½ teaspoon black pepper
½ cup (approximately)
    chicken broth
1½ teaspoons cornstarch
1 tablespoon chopped onion
1 tablespoon chopped red
    hot chili pepper
1 tablespoon minced cilantro

1. Place each chicken piece between two sheets of plastic wrap. Pound with mallet or rolling pin to flatten to ¼-inch thickness.

2. Combine lime juice, 1 tablespoon oil, lime peel, garlic, salt and black pepper in medium bowl. Add chicken; toss to coat well. Cover and refrigerate 15 minutes to 1 hour.

3. Drain chicken, reserving marinade. Combine marinade and enough chicken broth to make ¾ cup liquid. Whisk in cornstarch; set aside.

4. Heat remaining 2 teaspoons oil in wok or large skillet over high heat. Stir-fry onion and chili pepper 1 minute; remove from wok with slotted spoon. Set aside.

5. Cook chicken over medium-high heat 4 to 5 minutes or until lightly browned on bottom. Turn chicken and cook 4 to 5 minutes longer or until chicken is no longer pink in center. Remove chicken from wok; keep warm.

6. Combine broth mixture and onion mixture in wok. Boil sauce until thickened, scraping bottom of wok to loosen all drippings. Pour sauce over chicken; sprinkle with cilantro. *Makes 4 servings*

 Note: Seasoned stir-fry oils differ in "heat." If oil is extremely peppery, use 1 tablespoon vegetable oil and 2 teaspoons hot oil.

Chicken with Lime Sauce

SAUCY–SPICY TURKEY MEATBALLS

1 pound ground turkey
⅓ cup bread crumbs
1 egg
1 clove garlic, minced
1 teaspoon grated fresh
  ginger
¾ to 1 teaspoon red pepper
  flakes, divided
2 tablespoons light soy sauce,
  divided
1 tablespoon vegetable oil

1 can (20 ounces) pineapple
  chunks, undrained
1 tablespoon cornstarch
2 tablespoons lemon juice or
  orange juice
2 tablespoons honey
1 large red bell pepper,
  seeded and cut into
  1-inch triangles
Hot cooked rice

1. Combine turkey, bread crumbs, egg, garlic, ginger, ½ teaspoon red pepper flakes and 1 tablespoon soy sauce in large bowl. Shape turkey mixture into 1-inch meatballs.

2. Heat oil in wok or large skillet over medium-high heat. Add meatballs and cook 4 to 5 minutes or until no longer pink in centers, turning to brown all sides. Remove from wok.

3. Drain pineapple, reserving juice. Add enough water to juice to make 1 cup liquid. Whisk together pineapple juice mixture, cornstarch, lemon juice, honey, remaining 1 tablespoon soy sauce and ¼ teaspoon red pepper flakes. Pour into wok. Cook and stir until sauce thickens.

4. Add meatballs, pineapple and bell pepper to sauce. Cook and stir until hot. Adjust seasoning with remaining ¼ teaspoon red pepper flakes, if desired. Serve over rice.   *Makes 4 to 5 servings*

Saucy-Spicy Turkey Meatballs

MANDARIN ORANGE CHICKEN

2 tablespoons rice vinegar

2 tablespoons light soy sauce

2 tablespoons olive oil, divided

2 teaspoons grated orange peel

1 clove garlic, minced

1 pound boneless skinless chicken breasts, cut into strips

2 cans (11 ounces each) mandarin oranges, undrained

½ cup (approximately) orange juice

2 tablespoons cornstarch

½ teaspoon red pepper flakes

1 onion, cut into thin wedges

1 small zucchini, halved and sliced diagonally

1 small yellow squash, halved and sliced diagonally

1 red bell pepper, seeded and cut into 1-inch triangles

1 can (3 ounces) chow mein noodles (optional)

1. Combine vinegar, soy sauce, 1 tablespoon oil, orange peel and garlic in medium bowl. Add chicken; toss to coat well. Cover and refrigerate 15 minutes to 1 hour.

2. Drain chicken, reserving marinade. Drain oranges, reserving liquid; set oranges aside. Combine marinade from chicken and liquid from oranges in small bowl; add enough orange juice to make 2 cups liquid. Whisk in cornstarch and red pepper flakes; set aside.

3. Heat remaining 1 tablespoon oil in wok or large skillet over high heat. Add chicken; stir-fry 2 to 3 minutes or until no longer pink in center. Remove chicken; set aside.

4. Stir-fry onion 1 minute over high heat. Add zucchini and squash; stir-fry 1 minute. Add bell pepper; stir-fry 1 minute or until all vegetables are crisp-tender. Add orange juice mixture; stir until mixture comes to a boil. Add chicken, stirring until hot. Add oranges and gently stir. Transfer to serving plate. Top with chow mein noodles, if desired.

Makes 6 servings

MEDITERRANEAN TURKEY AND EGGPLANT STIR-FRY

1 pound ground turkey
1 cup onion, thinly sliced
2 cloves garlic, minced
1½ teaspoons dried oregano
  leaves
1 teaspoon dried mint leaves
¾ teaspoon salt
¼ teaspoon black pepper
4 cups eggplant cut into
  ½-inch cubes

1 green bell pepper, seeded
  and cut into ½-inch cubes
1 tablespoon olive oil
1 teaspoon sugar
1 medium tomato, peeled
  and cut into wedges*
2 tablespoons feta cheese,
  crumbled

To peel tomato, cut a skin-deep "x" in blossom end of the tomato. Drop into boiling water and blanch 15 seconds. Lift out with slotted spoon and drop into bowl of ice water. Skin will slip off easily.

1. In large nonstick skillet, over medium-high heat, sauté turkey, onion, garlic, oregano, mint, salt and pepper 5 to 6 minutes or until meat is no longer pink. Remove turkey mixture from skillet and set aside.

2. In same skillet, over medium-high heat, sauté eggplant and bell pepper in oil 4 minutes or until vegetables are crisp-tender.

3. Combine turkey mixture with vegetable mixture. Stir in sugar and tomato. Cook mixture, over medium-high heat, 4 to 5 minutes or until heated throughout.

4. To serve, top turkey mixture with feta cheese.

Makes 4 servings

Favorite recipe from **National Turkey Federation**

SELECTIONS FROM THE SEA

SHRIMP AND VEGETABLES WITH LO MEIN NOODLES

2 tablespoons vegetable oil
1 pound raw medium shrimp, peeled
2 packages (21 ounces each) frozen lo mein stir-fry mix with sauce

¼ cup peanuts
Fresh cilantro
1 small wedge cabbage

1. Heat oil in wok or large skillet over medium-high heat until hot. Add shrimp; stir-fry 3 minutes or until shrimp are pink and opaque. Remove from wok to medium bowl. Set aside.

2. Remove sauce packet from stir-fry mix. Add frozen vegetables and noodles to wok; stir in sauce. Cover and cook 7 to 8 minutes, stirring frequently.

3. While vegetable mixture is cooking, chop peanuts and enough cilantro to measure 2 tablespoons. Shred cabbage.

4. Stir shrimp, peanuts and cilantro into vegetable mixture; heat through. Serve immediately with cabbage. *Makes 6 servings*

Prep and Cook Time: 19 minutes

Shrimp and Vegetables with Lo Mein Noodles

SEARED SALMON TERIYAKI

¼ cup soy sauce
¼ cup sake
2 tablespoons sugar
1½ pounds red salmon fillet
    with skin (1¼ inches
    thick)
2 tablespoons vegetable oil,
    divided
2 medium zucchini (12
    ounces), cut into strips

2 medium yellow squash
    (12 ounces), cut into
    strips
1 tablespoon butter
¼ teaspoon salt
¼ teaspoon black pepper
1 tablespoon toasted sesame
    seeds
Lemon slices (optional)

1. Combine soy sauce, sake and sugar in cup; stir until sugar dissolves.

2. Rinse and dry salmon. Run fingers over cut surface of salmon; remove any bones that remain. Cut crosswise into 4 pieces.

3. Heat wok over high heat until hot. Add 1 tablespoon oil; heat 30 seconds. Add zucchini, yellow squash and butter. Cook and stir 4 to 5 minutes or until lightly browned and tender. Sprinkle squash mixture with salt and pepper. Transfer to serving platter. Sprinkle with sesame seeds; cover and keep warm.

4. Add remaining 1 tablespoon oil to wok and heat over high heat until sizzling hot. Carefully place fish in wok, skin sides up. Cook 4 minutes or until browned. Reduce heat to medium-high. Turn fish over using 2 pancake turners or flat spatulas. Cook, skin sides down, 8 to 10 minutes or until fish flakes easily when tested with fork, loosening fish on bottom occasionally. Place fish over squash mixture on platter. Cover and keep warm.

5. Pour off fat from wok. Stir soy sauce mixture and pour into wok. Boil until mixture is reduced by half and slightly thickened. Spoon sauce over fish. Serve with lemon, if desired.   *Makes 4 servings*

Seared Salmon Teriyaki

COMBINATION CHOP SUEY

2 whole chicken breasts
4 cups chicken broth
2 teaspoons cornstarch
1 cup water
4 teaspoons soy sauce
1 teaspoon instant chicken
  bouillon granules
3 tablespoons vegetable oil
8 ounces boneless lean pork,
  finely chopped
½ head bok choy or napa
  cabbage (about 8
  ounces), finely chopped

4 ounces fresh green beans,
  trimmed and cut into
  1-inch pieces
3 stalks celery, diagonally cut
  into ½-inch pieces
2 yellow onions, chopped
1 large carrot, chopped
8 ounces medium shrimp,
  peeled and deveined
1 can (8 ounces) sliced
  bamboo shoots, drained
Hot cooked rice (optional)

1. Combine chicken and chicken broth in large saucepan. Bring to a boil over medium-high heat. Reduce heat to low; cover. Simmer 20 to 30 minutes or until chicken is no longer pink in center. Remove from heat. Let stand until chicken is cool.

2. Remove skin and bones from chicken. Coarsely chop chicken.

3. Combine cornstarch, water, soy sauce and bouillon granules; set aside.

4. Heat oil in wok or large skillet over high heat. Add pork; stir-fry until no longer pink in center, about 5 minutes. Remove from wok; set aside.

5. Add cabbage, beans, celery, onions and carrot to wok; stir-fry until crisp-tender, about 3 minutes. Stir soy sauce mixture; add to wok. Cook and stir until liquid boils and thickens, about 3 minutes. Add chicken, shrimp, pork and bamboo shoots. Cook and stir until shrimp turn pink and are cooked through, about 3 minutes. Serve over hot cooked rice.   *Makes 4 to 6 servings*

Combination Chop Suey

SCALLOPS & SNOW PEAS

¾ pound fresh or thawed bay
   scallops
¾ cup water
2 tablespoons KIKKOMAN®
   Soy Sauce
2 tablespoons dry white wine
4 teaspoons cornstarch
½ teaspoon sugar
3 small dried whole red chili
   peppers

1 tablespoon vegetable oil
1 medium onion, cut into
   1-inch pieces
2 teaspoons slivered fresh
   ginger root
½ pound fresh snow peas,
   trimmed and cut
   diagonally in half
1½ teaspoons Oriental sesame
   oil

Cook scallops in small amount of boiling water 30 seconds; drain. Combine ¾ cup water, soy sauce, wine, cornstarch and sugar in small bowl; set aside. Cut each chili pepper open lengthwise, being careful not to cut all the way through; set aside. Heat vegetable oil in hot wok or large skillet over medium heat; add chilies and stir-fry 30 seconds. Remove chilies; increase heat to high. Add onion and ginger; stir-fry 1 minute. Add snow peas; stir-fry 2 minutes longer. Add scallops, chilies and soy sauce mixture; cook and stir until sauce boils and thickens. Remove from heat and stir in sesame oil. Serve immediately.   *Makes 4 servings*

HALIBUT WITH CILANTRO AND LIME

1 pound halibut, tuna or
   swordfish steaks
2 tablespoons fresh lime juice
¼ cup low-sodium soy sauce
1 teaspoon cornstarch
½ teaspoon minced fresh
   ginger

½ teaspoon vegetable oil
½ cup slivered red or yellow
   onion
2 cloves garlic, minced
¼ cup coarsely chopped
   cilantro

1. Cut halibut into 1-inch pieces; sprinkle with lime juice.

2. Blend soy sauce into cornstarch in cup until smooth. Stir in ginger.

3. Heat oil in wok or large nonstick skillet over medium heat. Add onion and garlic; stir-fry 2 minutes. Add halibut; stir-fry 2 minutes or until halibut is opaque.

4. Stir soy sauce mixture; add to wok. Stir-fry 30 seconds or until sauce boils and thickens. Sprinkle with cilantro. Garnish with lime wedges, if desired. *Makes 4 servings*

GOLDEN SEAFARERS STIR-FRY

1 can (16 ounces) cling peach slices in juice or light syrup

$\frac{1}{3}$ cup **KIKKOMAN®** Stir-Fry Sauce

1 teaspoon cornstarch

2 tablespoons vegetable oil, divided

$\frac{2}{3}$ cup large walnut pieces

1 clove garlic, minced

$\frac{1}{2}$ teaspoon grated fresh ginger root

$\frac{1}{2}$ pound medium-size raw shrimp, peeled and deveined

4 ounces fresh snow peas, trimmed

1 cup cherry tomatoes, cut into halves

$\frac{1}{4}$ cup sliced green onions

Hot cooked rice

Reserving $\frac{1}{3}$ cup liquid, drain peaches. Blend liquid with stir-fry sauce and cornstarch in small bowl; set aside. Heat 1 tablespoon oil in hot wok or large skillet over medium heat. Add walnuts, garlic and ginger; stir-fry 1 minute. Remove. Heat remaining 1 tablespoon oil in same pan over high heat. Add shrimp and stir-fry 1 minute; remove. Add snow peas and stir-fry 2 minutes; remove. Pour stir-fry sauce mixture into pan; cook and stir until thickened. Add shrimp, snow peas, peaches, tomatoes and green onions; cook and stir until shrimp and vegetables are coated with sauce and heated through. Stir in reserved walnut mixture. Serve with rice. *Makes 4 to 6 servings*

STIR-FRIED CRAB LEGS

**1½ pounds frozen Alaska king
 crab legs, thawed and
 drained**
3 green onions
½ cup water
2 tablespoons dry sherry
**2 tablespoons reduced-
 sodium soy sauce**

1 tablespoon cornstarch
1 teaspoon sugar
3 tablespoons vegetable oil
**1 piece fresh ginger (about
 1-inch square), sliced**
2 cloves garlic, minced
Lemon wedges

1. Soak crab legs in water 30 minutes to leach out some of salt brine used for packaging.

2. Meanwhile, cut off roots from green onions; discard. Cut green tops into 1-inch lengths; set aside.

3. Cut crab legs into 2-inch-long pieces with poultry scissors or cleaver.

4. Combine water, sherry, soy sauce, cornstarch and sugar in small bowl; blend well. Set aside.

5. Heat wok over high heat about 1 minute or until hot. Drizzle oil into wok and heat 15 seconds. Add ginger and stir-fry about 1 minute to flavor oil. Remove and discard ginger with fork. Add crab pieces and garlic. Stir-fry 5 minutes.

6. Stir cornstarch mixture and pour into wok. Add green onion pieces and toss. Cook and stir until sauce boils and thickens. Transfer to serving platter. Serve with lemon wedges.

Makes 3 to 4 servings

Note: To extract meat from legs, snip along each side of shell with scissors and lift out meat with skewer before serving. Reheat meat in wok for a few seconds. Or to save time, serve in the shell with seafood shell crackers. Have guests crack the shells and remove meat with small seafood forks.

Stir-Fried Crab Legs

MEXICAN SHRIMP WITH HOT CHILI PEPPER BUTTER

2 tablespoons extra-virgin olive oil, divided

2 cloves garlic, minced, divided

1 cup chopped onion, divided

2 pounds large shrimp, peeled and deveined, divided

1/3 cup chili powder, divided

1/4 teaspoon ground red pepper

1/2 cup butter or margarine

1/4 cup fresh lime juice

3/4 teaspoon salt

3 cups hot cooked white rice or yellow Spanish rice

Lime wedges

Heat large nonstick skillet over medium-high heat; add 1 tablespoon oil and heat 1 minute. Add 1 clove garlic; cook 15 seconds. Add 1/2 cup onion and half of shrimp. Sprinkle with half of chili powder; cook until shrimp are opaque. Set aside. Repeat with remaining oil, garlic, onion, shrimp and chili powder. Return reserved shrimp mixture to skillet; add butter, lime juice and salt. Cook until butter melts. Spoon shrimp mixture on rice; serve with lime.   *Makes 4 servings*

SPICY FISH FILLETS WITH LEMON

Grated peel of 1/2 SUNKIST® lemon

1 teaspoon toasted sesame seeds

1/4 teaspoon onion salt

1/8 teaspoon ground white pepper

1/8 teaspoon ground cumin

1/8 teaspoon paprika

1/8 teaspoon red pepper flakes (optional)

4 talapia or sole fillets (about 3/4 pound)

1 tablespoon vegetable oil

Fresh lemon wedges

In small bowl, combine lemon peel, sesame seeds, onion salt and spices. Sprinkle over and rub onto both sides of fish fillets. Heat oil in large nonstick skillet sprayed with nonstick cooking spray. Sauté fish over medium-high heat 3 minutes; turn fish and cook 2 to 3 minutes longer or until fish is opaque and flakes easily with fork. Serve with lemon wedges.   *Makes 2 to 4 servings*

Mexican Shrimp with Hot Chili Pepper Butter

CRUNCHY GARDEN DELIGHTS

COUNTRY GARDEN STIR–FRY WITH HERBED BUTTER

½ pound whole green beans, stemmed

4 medium carrots, diagonally sliced about ⅛ inch thick (about 2 cups)

2 cups fresh cauliflower florets

¼ cup butter or margarine, softened

1 tablespoon fresh lemon juice

1 tablespoon finely chopped parsley

½ teaspoon salt

1. Place ⅓ cup water in large nonstick skillet or wok. Add beans, carrots and cauliflower. Bring to a boil. Reduce heat, cover tightly and simmer 8 to 10 minutes or until crisp-tender.

2. Meanwhile, in small bowl, whisk together butter, lemon juice, parsley and salt; set aside.

3. When vegetables are crisp-tender, uncover and increase heat to high. Cook, stirring gently, until all liquid has evaporated. *(Be careful not to burn vegetables.)*

4. Remove from heat; toss gently with butter mixture.

Makes 4 side-dish servings

Country Garden Stir-Fry with Herbed Butter

216

VEGETARIAN STIR–FRY

1 bag (16 ounces) **BIRDS EYE**® frozen Mixed Vegetables*

2 tablespoons water

1 can (14 ounces) kidney beans, drained

1 jar (14 ounces) spaghetti sauce

½ teaspoon garlic powder

½ cup grated Parmesan cheese

Or, substitute your favorite Birds Eye® frozen vegetable combination.

• In large skillet, place vegetables and water.

• Cover; cook 7 to 10 minutes over medium heat. Uncover; stir in beans, spaghetti sauce and garlic powder; cook until heated through.

• Sprinkle with cheese. *Makes 4 servings*

Prep Time: 2 minutes
Cook Time: 12 to 15 minutes

 Serving Suggestion: Serve over hot cooked rice or pasta.

HOT AND SPICY SPINACH

1 red bell pepper, cut into 1-inch pieces

1 clove garlic, minced

1 pound fresh spinach, rinsed and chopped

1 tablespoon mustard

1 teaspoon lemon juice

¼ teaspoon red pepper flakes

1. Spray large skillet with nonstick cooking spray; heat over medium heat. Add bell pepper and garlic; cook and stir 3 minutes.

2. Add spinach; cook and stir 3 minutes or just until spinach begins to wilt.

3. Stir in mustard, lemon juice and red pepper flakes. Serve immediately. *Makes 4 servings*

Vegetarian Stir-Fry

SZECHUAN VEGETABLE STIR–FRY

8 ounces firm tofu, drained and cut into cubes

1 cup vegetable broth, divided

½ cup orange juice

⅓ cup soy sauce

1 to 2 teaspoons hot chili oil

½ teaspoon fennel seeds

½ teaspoon ground black pepper

2 tablespoons cornstarch

3 tablespoons vegetable oil

1 cup sliced green onions and tops

3 medium carrots, diagonally sliced

3 cloves garlic, minced

2 teaspoons minced fresh ginger

¼ pound button mushrooms, sliced

1 medium red bell pepper, cut into 1-inch squares

¼ pound fresh snow peas, trimmed and cut diagonally into halves

8 ounces broccoli florets, steamed

½ cup peanuts

4 to 6 cups hot cooked rice

1. To marinate tofu, place in 8-inch round or square glass baking dish. Combine ½ cup vegetable broth, orange juice, soy sauce, chili oil, fennel seeds and black pepper in small bowl; pour over tofu. Let stand 15 to 60 minutes. Drain; reserve marinade.

2. Combine cornstarch and remaining ½ cup vegetable broth in medium bowl. Add reserved marinade; set aside.

3. Heat vegetable oil in wok or large skillet over high heat until hot. Add onions, carrots, garlic and ginger; stir-fry 3 minutes. Add tofu, mushrooms, bell pepper and snow peas; stir-fry 2 to 3 minutes or until vegetables are crisp-tender. Add broccoli; stir-fry 1 minute or until heated through.

4. Stir cornstarch mixture. Add to wok and cook 1 to 2 minutes or until bubbly. Stir in peanuts. Serve over rice.

Makes 4 to 6 servings

Szechuan Vegetable Stir-Fry

GREEN BEANS AND SHIITAKE MUSHROOMS

10 to 12 dried shiitake
   mushrooms (about
   1 ounce)
1/3 cup fresh basil leaves or
   chopped cilantro
3 tablespoons oyster sauce
1 tablespoon cornstarch
4 cloves garlic, minced

1/8 teaspoon red pepper flakes
1 tablespoon vegetable oil
3/4 to 1 pound fresh green
   beans, ends trimmed
2 green onions, cut diagonally
   into thin slices
1/3 cup roasted peanuts
   (optional)

1. Place mushrooms in bowl; cover with hot water. Let stand 30 minutes or until caps are soft. Drain mushrooms; squeeze out excess water. Remove and discard stems. Slice caps into thin strips.

2. Break off and discard stems from basil. Rinse leaves; pat dry with paper towels. Layer some of leaves on cutting board with largest leaf on bottom, then roll up jelly-roll fashion. Slice roll into 1/4-inch-thick slices; separate into strips. Repeat with remaining basil.

3. Combine 1/4 cup water, oyster sauce, cornstarch, garlic and pepper flakes in small bowl; mix well. Set aside.

4. Heat wok or medium skillet over medium-high heat. Add oil and swirl to coat surface. Add mushrooms, beans and 1/2 cup water; cook and stir until water boils. Reduce heat to medium-low; cover and cook 8 to 10 minutes or until beans are crisp-tender, stirring occasionally.

5. Stir cornstarch mixture; add to wok. Cook and stir until sauce thickens and coats beans. (If cooking water has evaporated, add enough water to form thick sauce.)

6. Stir in green onions, basil and peanuts, if desired; mix well. Transfer to serving platter. Garnish as desired.   *Makes 4 to 6 servings*

Green Beans and Shiitake Mushrooms

SWEET 'N SOUR STIR-FRY

2 tablespoons vegetable oil
1 cup thinly sliced carrots
1 cup snow peas
1 small green bell pepper, cut into chunks
1 medium tomato, cut into wedges
1 cup sliced water chestnuts

½ cup sliced cucumber, cut into halves
¾ cup **WISH-BONE**® Sweet 'n Spicy French Dressing*
2 tablespoons packed brown sugar
2 teaspoons soy sauce
Sesame seeds (optional)

Also terrific with Wish-Bone® Russian Dressing.

In medium skillet, heat oil over medium heat; cook carrots, snow peas and bell pepper, stirring frequently, 5 minutes or until crisp-tender. Add tomato, water chestnuts, cucumber and Sweet 'n Spicy French Dressing blended with brown sugar and soy sauce. Simmer 5 minutes or until vegetables are tender. Top with sesame seeds, if desired.   *Makes about 6 servings*

ZUCCHINI SHANGHAI STYLE

4 dried Chinese black mushrooms
½ cup defatted low-sodium chicken broth
2 tablespoons ketchup
2 teaspoons dry sherry
1 teaspoon low-sodium soy sauce
1 teaspoon red wine vinegar
¼ teaspoon sugar
1½ teaspoons vegetable oil, divided

1 teaspoon minced fresh ginger
1 clove garlic, minced
1 large tomato, peeled, seeded and chopped
1 green onion, finely chopped
1 teaspoon cornstarch
1 pound zucchini (about 3 medium), diagonally cut into 1-inch pieces
½ small yellow onion, cut into wedges and separated

1. Soak mushrooms in warm water 20 minutes. Drain, reserving ¼ cup liquid. Squeeze out excess water. Discard stems; slice caps. Combine reserved ¼ cup mushroom liquid, chicken broth, ketchup, sherry, soy sauce, vinegar and sugar in small bowl.

2. Heat 1 teaspoon oil in large saucepan over medium heat. Add ginger and garlic; stir-fry 10 seconds. Add mushrooms, tomato and green onion; stir-fry 1 minute. Add chicken broth mixture; bring to a boil over high heat. Reduce heat to medium; simmer 10 minutes.

3. Combine 1 tablespoon water and cornstarch in small bowl. Heat remaining ½ teaspoon oil in large nonstick skillet over medium heat. Add zucchini and yellow onion; stir-fry 30 seconds. Add 3 tablespoons water. Cover and cook 3 to 4 minutes or until vegetables are crisp-tender, stirring occasionally. Add tomato mixture to skillet. Stir cornstarch mixture and add to skillet. Cook until sauce boils and thickens. *Makes 4 side-dish servings*

SESAME BROCCOLI

1½ **pounds fresh broccoli,**
    trimmed
    Boiling water
¼ **cup KIKKOMAN® Stir-Fry**
    Sauce
¾ **teaspoon Oriental sesame**
    oil

2 **tablespoons vegetable oil**
1 **tablespoon slivered fresh**
    ginger root
2 **teaspoons sesame seed,**
    toasted

Remove flowerets from broccoli; cut into bite-size pieces. Peel stalks; cut crosswise into ¼-inch slices. Place in medium bowl; pour in enough boiling water to cover and let stand 2 minutes. Drain; cool on several layers of paper towels. Combine stir-fry sauce and sesame oil; set aside. Heat vegetable oil in hot wok or large skillet over medium-high heat. Add broccoli and ginger; stir-fry 3 minutes. Add stir-fry sauce mixture; cook and stir until broccoli is coated with sauce. Transfer to serving platter and sprinkle sesame seed evenly over broccoli. *Makes 6 servings*

PORTOBELLO STIR-FRY WITH BLUE CHEESE

8 ounces uncooked fusilli
    pasta
1 pound stemmed portobello
    mushrooms, cleaned and
    cut into ½-inch slices
½ cup extra-virgin olive oil

3 tablespoons lemon juice
2 cloves garlic, minced
½ teaspoon dry mustard
¾ teaspoon salt
¼ teaspoon black pepper
¼ cup crumbled blue cheese

Cook pasta according to package directions. Place mushrooms in 13×9-inch glass dish. Whisk together oil, lemon juice, garlic, mustard, salt and pepper. Pour over mushrooms; marinate 10 minutes.* Heat large nonstick skillet over medium-high heat. Add half of mushrooms in single layer. Cook 4 minutes on both sides or until mushrooms begin to brown. Place pasta on serving platter. Top with mushrooms; cover. Repeat with remaining mushrooms and add to pasta; top with blue cheese.   *Makes 4 servings*

Mushrooms begin to break down after 10 minutes.

GOLDEN COINS
(SESAME STIR-FRIED CARROTS)

⅓ cup KIKKOMAN® Stir-Fry
    Sauce
2 tablespoons water
2 tablespoons vegetable oil
1½ pounds carrots, peeled and
    cut crosswise into ⅛-inch
    slices

1 tablespoon minced fresh
    ginger root
1 tablespoon sesame seed,
    toasted
1½ teaspoons Oriental sesame
    oil

Blend stir-fry sauce and water; set aside. Heat vegetable oil in hot wok or large skillet over high heat. Add carrots and ginger; reduce heat to medium-high and stir-fry 5 minutes. Add stir-fry sauce mixture. Cook, stirring, until carrots are coated with sauce. Remove from heat; stir in sesame seed and sesame oil. Serve immediately.
                                    Makes 6 servings

Portobello Stir-Fry with Blue Cheese

Rice & Noodle Favorites

FRUITED WILD RICE WITH TOASTED NUTS

2 boxes (6.2 ounces each) fast-cooking long grain and wild rice

2 tablespoons walnut or vegetable oil, divided

1 package (2½ ounces) walnut pieces or ⅔ cup almond slivers

1 package (2¼ ounces) pecan pieces

2 cups chopped onions

12 dried apricots, sliced (about ½ cup)

½ cup dried cherries or dried cranberries

2 teaspoons minced fresh ginger

¼ teaspoon red pepper flakes

¼ cup honey

3 tablespoons soy sauce

1 tablespoon grated orange peel

Cook rice according to package directions.

Add 1 tablespoon oil to large nonstick skillet or wok. Heat skillet over medium-high heat 1 minute. Add walnuts and pecans; cook, stirring frequently, 8 minutes or until pecans are browned. Remove from skillet and set aside. Add remaining 1 tablespoon oil and onions to skillet; cook 10 minutes or until onions begin to brown. Add apricots, cherries, ginger, pepper and reserved nuts; cook 5 minutes. Whisk together honey, soy sauce and orange peel in small bowl; add to onion mixture. Toss with rice.   *Makes 4 servings*

Fruited Wild Rice with Toasted Nuts

THIN NOODLES WITH CHICKEN AND VEGETABLES

6 ounces (about 3 cups) uncooked thin noodles or bean threads
½ cup chicken broth
2 tablespoons hoisin sauce
1 tablespoon vegetable oil
2 green onions, finely chopped
1 teaspoon minced fresh ginger

1 clove garlic, minced
1 pound boneless skinless chicken breasts, cut into bite-size pieces
1 package frozen vegetable medley, thawed and drained*
¼ cup orange marmalade
2 tablespoons chili sauce
¼ teaspoon red pepper flakes

*Use your favorite medley such as cauliflower, carrots and snow peas.

1. Place 6 cups water in wok; bring to a boil. Add noodles; cook 3 minutes or until *al dente*. Drain. Place in medium bowl; stir in chicken broth and hoisin sauce. Set aside; keep warm.

2. Heat oil in wok or large skillet over high heat. Add onions, ginger and garlic; stir-fry 15 seconds. Add chicken; stir-fry 3 to 4 minutes or until almost done. Add vegetables; stir-fry until vegetables are hot and chicken is no longer pink in center. Add marmalade, chili sauce and pepper. Stir until hot. Serve over noodles. *Makes 4 servings*

LEE KUM KEE® FRIED RICE

2 tablespoons vegetable oil
2 eggs, beaten
2 cups cooled cooked rice
½ pound diced cooked chicken
½ cup mixed vegetables

5 tablespoons **LEE KUM KEE**® Oyster Flavored Sauce
1 tablespoon diced green onion

Heat skillet over medium heat. Add oil. Add egg and scramble. Stir in rice, chicken, vegetables and Oyster Flavored Sauce. Stir-fry until heated through. Sprinkle with onion. *Makes 4 servings*

Thin Noodles with Chicken and Vegetables

JAMBALAYA STIR–FRY ON CAJUN RICE

1 cup uncooked converted rice

2 teaspoons chicken bouillon granules

1 can (16 ounces) diced tomatoes, undrained

½ cup finely chopped celery

1 bay leaf

8 ounces andouille sausage, cut in ¼-inch rounds*

1½ cups chopped onions

1 cup chopped green bell pepper

½ pound raw large shrimp, peeled and deveined

½ pound boneless chicken breasts, cut into 1-inch pieces

¾ teaspoon dried thyme leaves

¼ cup chopped parsley

1 teaspoon salt

½ teaspoon ground red pepper

½ teaspoon paprika

Hot pepper sauce

*If unavailable, use kielbasa sausage.

1. Bring 1¾ cups water to a boil in medium saucepan. Add rice, bouillon granules, tomatoes and their liquid, celery and bay leaf. Return to a boil; reduce heat and cover tightly. Simmer 20 minutes or until all liquid is absorbed.

2. Meanwhile, heat large skillet over medium-high heat 1 minute. Add sausage, onions and bell pepper; cook and stir 10 minutes.

3. Increase heat to high; add shrimp, chicken and thyme. Cook and stir 5 minutes. Add parsley, salt, ground red pepper and paprika. Stir to blend thoroughly.

4. Remove bay leaf from rice; discard. Place rice on platter. Spoon shrimp mixture over rice and serve with pepper sauce.

Makes 4 servings

Jambalaya Stir-Fry on Cajun Rice

EGG NOODLES AND VEGETABLES WITH PESTO

1 package (16 ounces) enriched fine egg noodles
5 tablespoons olive oil, divided
10 cloves garlic
3 cups fresh basil leaves, lightly packed
3 cups fresh spinach, lightly packed
1/2 cup bottled fat-free Italian salad dressing

4 cups broccoli florets
4 cups cauliflower florets
2 large onions, cut into strips
2 cups sliced mushrooms
1/2 teaspoon red pepper flakes
2 pints cherry tomatoes, cut into halves
1/2 cup shredded Asiago cheese

1. Cook noodles according to package directions, taking care not to overcook. Drain; place in large bowl. Toss with 1 tablespoon oil.

2. To make pesto, place garlic in food processor; process briefly until chopped. Add basil; process using on/off pulsing action until finely chopped. Transfer to medium bowl. Process spinach until finely chopped. Add 3 tablespoons oil and salad dressing; process briefly to blend. Add to basil mixture in bowl.

3. Heat remaining 1 tablespoon oil in large nonstick skillet or wok over medium heat until hot. Add broccoli, cauliflower and onions. Cover and cook 5 minutes, stirring occasionally. Add mushrooms and pepper; cook, uncovered, 5 minutes or until vegetables are crisp-tender. Add vegetable mixture, tomatoes and pesto to noodles; toss until well blended. Serve with cheese. Garnish with fresh basil, if desired.

Makes 8 servings

Egg Noodles and Vegetables with Pesto

TURKEY AND ORZO IN CILANTRO MUSTARD

1 cup orzo pasta
1 tablespoon butter or
    margarine
1 tablespoon olive oil
1 small onion, minced
2 cloves garlic, minced
1 package (about 1¼ pounds)
    PERDUE® FIT 'N EASY®
    Fresh Skinless & Boneless
    Thin-Sliced Turkey or
    Chicken Breast Cutlets,
    cut into thin strips

4 tablespoons chopped fresh
    cilantro, divided
2 tablespoons Dijon mustard
½ cup freshly grated
    Parmesan cheese

Cook orzo in boiling water according to package directions, about 10 minutes or until *al dente;* drain. Meanwhile, in large skillet over medium-high heat, heat butter and oil until butter melts. Add onion and garlic; sauté 1 minute. Add turkey; sauté about 2 minutes or until almost cooked through. Add 2 tablespoons water; cook 1 minute. Stir in 2 tablespoons cilantro and mustard. In serving bowl, toss orzo with turkey mixture and cheese. To serve, garnish with remaining 2 tablespoons cilantro.   *Makes 4 to 6 servings*

Prep Time: 5 minutes
Cook Time: 12 minutes

ALMOND FRIED RICE

2 tablespoons vegetable oil
¾ cup thinly sliced green
    onions and tops
½ cup diced red bell pepper
1 egg, beaten
3 cups cold, cooked rice

2 ounces diced cooked ham
    (about ½ cup)
2 tablespoons KIKKOMAN®
    Soy Sauce
½ cup slivered blanched
    almonds, toasted

Heat oil in hot wok or large skillet over medium-high heat. Add green onions and bell pepper; stir-fry 1 minute. Add egg and scramble. Stir in rice and cook until heated through, gently separating grains. Add ham and soy sauce; cook and stir until mixture is well blended. Just before serving, stir in almonds.

Makes 4 servings

THAI PEANUT NOODLE STIR-FRY

1 cup chicken broth or low-sodium chicken broth
½ cup **GREY POUPON®** Dijon Mustard
⅓ cup creamy peanut butter
3 tablespoons firmly packed light brown sugar
2 tablespoons soy sauce
1 clove garlic, crushed
½ teaspoon minced fresh ginger
1 tablespoon cornstarch
4 cups cut-up vegetables (red bell pepper, carrot, mushrooms, green onions, pea pods)
1 tablespoon vegetable oil
1 pound linguine, cooked
Chopped peanuts and scallion brushes for garnish

In medium saucepan, combine chicken broth, mustard, peanut butter, sugar, soy sauce, garlic, ginger and cornstarch. Cook over medium heat until mixture thickens and begins to boil; reduce heat and keep warm.

In large skillet, over medium-high heat, sauté vegetables in oil until tender, about 5 minutes. In large serving bowl, combine hot cooked pasta, vegetables and peanut sauce, tossing until well coated. Garnish with chopped peanuts and scallion brushes. Serve immediately.

Makes 4 to 6 servings

TWO CHEESE MEDITERRANEAN STIR-FRY

6 ounces uncooked penne pasta

2 tablespoons extra-virgin olive oil, divided

4 cloves garlic, minced

½ pound fresh whole mushrooms, cut into quarters

2 cups diced eggplant

1½ cups zucchini cut into matchstick-size strips

1 green bell pepper, cut into 1-inch pieces

1 cup chopped onion

1½ teaspoons dried basil leaves

¾ teaspoon salt or to taste

⅛ teaspoon black pepper

4 plum tomatoes, cut into quarters and seeded

2 to 3 tablespoons capers, well drained (optional)

3 ounces provolone cheese, shredded

¼ cup grated Parmesan cheese, divided

1. Cook pasta according to package directions.

2. Meanwhile, place 1 tablespoon oil in large nonstick skillet or wok. Heat over medium-high heat 1 minute. Add garlic; cook 1 minute. Add mushrooms, eggplant, zucchini, bell pepper, onion, basil, salt and black pepper. Cook 15 minutes or until eggplant is tender.

3. Gently stir in tomatoes and capers, if desired. Reduce heat; cover tightly and simmer 5 minutes.

4. Remove skillet from heat; toss with remaining 1 tablespoon oil, provolone cheese and 2 tablespoons Parmesan cheese.

5. Place cooked pasta on serving platter. Spoon vegetable mixture over pasta and top with remaining 2 tablespoons Parmesan cheese.

Makes 4 servings

Two Cheese Mediterranean Stir-Fry

ORZO WITH CHICKEN AND CABBAGE

8 ounces orzo pasta
¼ cup rice vinegar
¼ cup chicken broth
2 tablespoons packed brown
   sugar
2 tablespoons soy sauce
1 teaspoon cornstarch
1 tablespoon sesame chili oil
2 cups thinly sliced red
   cabbage
1 tablespoon seasoned
   stir-fry or hot oil

1 pound boneless skinless
   chicken breasts or
   tenders, cut into bite-size
   pieces
4 ounces snow peas
4 green onions with tops
   (separating white and
   green parts), sliced into
   ½-inch pieces
1 tablespoon sesame seeds,
   toasted

1. Place 6 cups water in wok or large saucepan; bring to a boil over high heat. Add orzo; cook according to package directions until *al dente*, stirring occasionally. Drain; set aside.

2. Whisk together vinegar, chicken broth, brown sugar, soy sauce and cornstarch in small bowl; set aside.

3. Heat sesame chili oil in wok or large skillet over high heat. Add cabbage; stir-fry 2 to 3 minutes or until crisp-tender. Remove. Set aside on serving platter; keep warm.

4. Heat stir-fry oil in same wok over high heat. Add chicken; stir-fry 3 minutes. Add snow peas and white parts of green onions; stir-fry 1 to 2 minutes or until vegetables are crisp-tender. Add vinegar mixture, stirring until hot and slightly thickened. Add orzo and toss. Serve over cabbage. Sprinkle with green onion tops and sesame seeds.

Makes 4 servings

My Favorites

My Favorite Recipes

Favorite recipe: _____

Favorite recipe from: _____

Ingredients: _____

_____

_____

_____

_____

_____

Method: _____

_____

_____

_____

_____

_____

_____

_____

_____

_____

_____

My Favorite Recipes

Favorite recipe: _____

Favorite recipe from: _____

Ingredients: _____

_____

_____

_____

_____

Method: _____

_____

_____

_____

_____

_____

_____

_____

_____

_____

My Favorite Recipes

Favorite recipe: _____

Favorite recipe from: _____

Ingredients: _____

_____

_____

_____

_____

_____

Method: _____

_____

_____

_____

_____

_____

_____

_____

_____

_____

_____

My Favorite Recipes

Favorite recipe: _____

Favorite recipe from: _____

Ingredients: _____

_____

_____

_____

_____

Method: _____

_____

_____

_____

_____

_____

_____

_____

_____

_____

My Favorite Recipes

Favorite recipe: _____

Favorite recipe from: _____

Ingredients: _____

_____

_____

_____

_____

_____

Method: _____

_____

_____

_____

_____

_____

_____

_____

_____

_____

_____

_____

My Favorite Recipes

Favorite recipe: _____

Favorite recipe from: _____

Ingredients: _____

_____

_____

_____

_____

_____

Method: _____

_____

_____

_____

_____

_____

_____

_____

_____

_____

_____

My Favorite Recipes

Favorite recipe: _____

Favorite recipe from: _____

Ingredients: _____

_____

_____

_____

_____

Method: _____

_____

_____

_____

_____

_____

_____

_____

_____

My Favorite Recipes

Favorite recipe: _____

Favorite recipe from: _____

Ingredients: _____

_____

_____

_____

_____

Method: _____

_____

_____

_____

_____

_____

_____

_____

_____

_____

My Favorite Recipes

Favorite recipe: _____

Favorite recipe from: _____

Ingredients: _____

_____

_____

_____

_____

Method: _____

_____

_____

_____

_____

_____

_____

_____

_____

My Favorite Recipes

Favorite recipe: _____

Favorite recipe from: _____

Ingredients: _____

_____

_____

_____

_____

_____

Method: _____

_____

_____

_____

_____

_____

_____

_____

_____

_____

_____

_____

My Favorite Recipes

Favorite recipe: _____

Favorite recipe from: _____

Ingredients: _____

_____

_____

_____

_____

_____

Method: _____

_____

_____

_____

_____

_____

_____

_____

_____

_____

_____

My Favorite Recipes

Favorite recipe: _____

Favorite recipe from: _____

Ingredients: _____

_____

_____

_____

_____

_____

Method: _____

_____

_____

_____

_____

_____

_____

_____

_____

_____

_____

My Favorite Recipes

Favorite recipe: _____

Favorite recipe from: _____

Ingredients: _____

_____

_____

_____

_____

_____

Method: _____

_____

_____

_____

_____

_____

_____

_____

_____

_____

_____

My Favorite Recipes

Favorite recipe: _____

Favorite recipe from: _____

Ingredients: _____

_____

_____

_____

_____

_____

Method: _____

_____

_____

_____

_____

_____

_____

_____

_____

_____

_____

My Favorite Recipes

Favorite recipe: _____

Favorite recipe from: _____

Ingredients: _____

_____

_____

_____

_____

_____

Method: _____

_____

_____

_____

_____

_____

_____

_____

_____

_____

My Favorite Recipes

Favorite recipe: _____

Favorite recipe from: _____

Ingredients: _____

_____

_____

_____

_____

_____

Method: _____

_____

_____

_____

_____

_____

_____

_____

_____

_____

_____

_____

My Favorite Recipes

Favorite recipe: _____

Favorite recipe from: _____

Ingredients: _____

_____

_____

_____

_____

_____

Method: _____

_____

_____

_____

_____

_____

_____

_____

_____

_____

My Favorite Recipes

Favorite recipe: _____

Favorite recipe from: _____

Ingredients: _____

_____

_____

_____

_____

_____

Method: _____

_____

_____

_____

_____

_____

_____

_____

_____

_____

_____

_____

My Favorite Recipes

Favorite recipe: _____

Favorite recipe from: _____

Ingredients: _____

_____

_____

_____

_____

_____

Method: _____

_____

_____

_____

_____

_____

_____

_____

_____

_____

_____

My Favorite Recipes

Favorite recipe: _____

Favorite recipe from: _____

Ingredients: _____

_____

_____

_____

_____

_____

Method: _____

_____

_____

_____

_____

_____

_____

_____

_____

_____

_____

My Favorite Dinner Party

Date: _____

Occasion: _____

_____

Guests: _____

_____

_____

_____

Menu: _____

_____

_____

_____

_____

_____

_____

_____

_____

_____

My Favorite Dinner Party

Date: _____

Occasion: _____

_____

Guests: _____

_____

_____

_____

_____

Menu: _____

_____

_____

_____

_____

_____

_____

_____

_____

_____

My Favorite Dinner Party

Date: _____

Occasion: _____
_____

Guests: _____
_____
_____
_____
_____

Menu: _____
_____
_____
_____
_____
_____
_____
_____
_____
_____
_____
_____

My Favorite Dinner Party

Date: _____

Occasion: _____

_____

Guests: _____

_____

_____

_____

_____

Menu: _____

_____

_____

_____

_____

_____

_____

_____

_____

_____

_____

My Favorite Brunch

Date: _____

Occasion: _____
_____

Guests: _____
_____
_____
_____

Menu: _____
_____
_____
_____
_____
_____
_____
_____
_____
_____

My Favorite Brunch

Date: _____

Occasion: _____

_____

Guests: _____

_____

_____

_____

Menu: _____

_____

_____

_____

_____

_____

_____

_____

_____

_____

My Favorite Brunch

Date: _____

Occasion: _____

_____

Guests: _____

_____

_____

_____

Menu: _____

_____

_____

_____

_____

_____

_____

_____

_____

_____

_____

_____

My Favorite Brunch

Date: _____

Occasion: _____
_____

Guests: _____
_____
_____
_____
_____

Menu: _____
_____
_____
_____
_____
_____
_____
_____
_____
_____
_____
_____

My Favorite Food Gifts

Friend: _____

Date: _____

Food Gift: _____

_____

_____

_____

Friend: _____

Date: _____

Food Gift: _____

_____

_____

_____

Friend: _____

Date: _____

Food Gift: _____

_____

_____

_____

My Favorite Food Gifts

Friend: _____

Date: _____

Food Gift: _____

_____

_____

_____

Friend: _____

Date: _____

Food Gift: _____

_____

_____

_____

Friend: _____

Date: _____

Food Gift: _____

_____

_____

_____

My Favorite Friends

Friend: _____

Favorite foods: _____
_____

Don't serve: _____
_____
_____

Friend: _____

Favorite foods: _____
_____

Don't serve: _____
_____
_____

Friend: _____

Favorite foods: _____
_____

Don't serve: _____
_____
_____

My Favorite Friends

Friend: _____

Favorite foods: _____

_____

Don't serve: _____

_____

_____

Friend: _____

Favorite foods: _____

_____

Don't serve: _____

_____

_____

Friend: _____

Favorite foods: _____

_____

Don't serve: _____

_____

_____

Hints, Tips & Index

Casserole Cookware

Casserole cookware comes in a variety of shapes, sizes and materials that fall into 2 general descriptions. They can be either deep, round containers with handles and tight-fitting lids or square and rectangular baking dishes. Casseroles are made out of glass, ceramic or metal. When making a casserole, it's important to bake the casserole in the proper size dish so that the ingredients cook evenly in the time specified.

Size Unknown?

If the size of the casserole or baking dish isn't marked on the bottom of the dish, it can be measured to determine the size.

• Round and oval casseroles are measured by volume, not inches, and are always listed by quart capacity. Fill a measuring cup with water and pour it into an empty casserole. Repeat until the casserole is filled with water, keeping track of the amount of water added. The amount of water is equivalent to the size of the dish.

• Square and rectangular baking dishes are usually measured in inches. If the dimensions aren't marked on the bottom of a square or rectangular baking dish, use a ruler to measure on top from the inside of one edge to the inside of the edge across.

Helpful Preparation Techniques

Some of the recipes call for advance preparations, such as cooked chicken or pasta. In order to ensure success when following and preparing the recipes, here are several preparation tips and techniques.

• Tips for Cooking Pasta

For every pound of pasta, bring 4 to 6 quarts of water to a full, rolling boil. Gradually add pasta, allowing water to return to a boil. Stir frequently to prevent the pasta from sticking together.

Pasta is finished cooking when it is tender but still firm to the bite, or al dente. The pasta continues to cook when the casserole is placed in the oven so it is important that the pasta be slightly undercooked. Otherwise, the more the pasta cooks, the softer it becomes and, eventually, it will fall apart.

Immediately drain pasta to prevent overcooking. For best results, combine pasta with other ingredients immediately after draining.

• Tips for Cooking Rice
The different types of rice require different amounts of water and cooking times. Follow the package instructions for the best results.

Measure the amount of water specified on the package and pour into a medium saucepan. Bring to a boil over medium-high heat. Slowly add rice and return to a boil. Reduce heat to low. Cover and simmer for the time specified on the package or until the rice is tender and most of the water has been absorbed.

To test the rice for doneness, bite into a grain or squeeze a grain between your thumb and index finger. The rice is done when it is tender and the center is not hard.

• Tips for Chopping and Storing Fresh Herbs
To chop fresh herbs, place in glass measuring cup. Snip herbs into small pieces with kitchen scissors.

Wrap remaining fresh herbs in a slightly damp paper towel and place in an airtight plastic food storage bag. Store up to 5 days in the refrigerator.

Top it Off!
Buttery, golden brown bread crumbs are a popular choice when it comes to topping a casserole but the selections shouldn't end there. Be creative with the many choices available to jazz up an old favorite or just vary how they are used. Crispy toppings can be crushed, partially crushed, broken into bite-size pieces or left whole. Fruits, vegetables and other toppings

can be chopped, sliced or shredded. Sprinkle a new spice or herb in place of another one. All the toppings can be placed on top of the casserole in a variety of ways–a small amount in the center, around the edges as a border or in straight or diagonal lines across the top.

Crispy toppings add a nice texture to your casseroles. Choose from crushed unsweetened cereals; potato, corn, tortilla or bagel chips; pretzels; flour or corn tortilla strips; plain or flavored croutons; flavored crackers; crumbled bacon; ramen or chow mein noodles; sesame seeds; French fried onions and various nuts. As a guide, add 1 tablespoon melted margarine to ½ cup crushed crumbs. Sprinkle over casserole and bake to add buttery flavor.

Fruits, vegetables and other toppings add a burst of color to most casseroles. Add green, red or white onions; orange or lemon peel; mushrooms; dried or fresh fruits, such as apples, apricots, cranberries, dates, oranges, pineapple and raisins; olives; bell or chili peppers; bean sprouts; tomatoes; avocados; celery; corn; coconut; carrots; fresh herbs and shredded cheeses according to what flavor and look you desire. In order to keep the fruits and vegetables bright and crisp, add them 5 minutes before the casserole is finished cooking or sprinkle them on after it's out of the oven.

• Homemade Bread Crumbs

Making your own bread crumbs is a great way to use up the rest of a fresh loaf. To make bread crumbs, preheat oven to 300°F. Place a single layer of bread slices on a baking sheet and bake 5 to 8 minutes or until completely dry and lightly browned. Cool completely. Process in food processor or crumble in resealable plastic food storage bag until very fine. For additional flavor, season with salt, pepper and a small amount of dried herbs, ground spices or grated cheese as desired. Generally, 1 slice of bread equals ⅓ cup bread crumbs.

The Basics

• As with conventional cooking recipes, slow cooker recipe time ranges are provided to account for variables such as temperature of ingredients before cooking, how full the slow cooker is and even altitude. Once you become familiar with your slow cooker you'll have a good idea which end of the time range to use.

• Manufacturers recommend that slow cookers should be one-half to three-quarters full for best results.

• Keep a lid on it! The slow cooker can take as long as twenty minutes to regain the heat lost when the cover is removed. If the recipe calls for stirring or checking the dish near the end of the cooking time, replace the lid as quickly as you can.

• To clean your slow cooker, follow the manufacturer's instructions. To make cleanup even easier, spray with nonstick cooking spray before adding food.

• Always taste the finished dish before serving and adjust seasonings to your preference. Consider adding a dash of any of the following: salt, pepper, seasoned salt, seasoned herb blends, lemon juice, soy sauce, Worcestershire sauce, flavored vinegar, freshly ground pepper or minced fresh herbs.

TIPS & TECHNIQUES

Adapting Recipes

If you'd like to adapt your own favorite recipe to a slow cooker, you'll need to follow a few guidelines. First, try to find a similar recipe in this publication or your manufacturer's guide. Note the cooking times, liquid, quantity and size of meat and vegetable pieces. Because the slow cooker captures moisture, you will want to reduce the amount of liquid, often by as much as half. Add dairy products toward the end of the cooking time so they do not curdle.

Selecting the Right Meat

A good tip to keep in mind while shopping is that you can, and in fact should, use tougher, inexpensive cuts of meat. Top-quality cuts, such as loin chops or filet mignon, fall apart during long cooking periods. Keep those for roasting, broiling or grilling and save money when you use your slow cooker. You will be amazed to find even the toughest cuts come out fork-tender and flavorful.

Reducing Fat

The slow cooker can help you make meals lower in fat because you won't be cooking in fat as you do when you stir-fry and sauté. And tougher cuts of meat have less fat than prime cuts.

If you do use fatty cuts, such as ribs, consider browning them first on top of the range to cook off excess fat.

Chicken skin tends to shrivel and curl in the slow cooker; therefore, most recipes call for skinless chicken. If you use skin-on pieces, brown them before adding them to the slow cooker. If you would rather remove the skin, use the following technique: Freeze chicken until firm, but not hard. (Do not refreeze thawed chicken.) Grasp skin with clean cotton kitchen towel or paper towel and pull away from meat; discard skin. When finished skinning chicken, launder towel before using again.

You can easily remove most of the fat from accumulated juices, soups and canned broths. The simplest way is to refrigerate the liquid for several hours or overnight. The fat will congeal and float to the top for easy removal. If you plan to use the liquid right away, ladle it into a bowl or measuring cup. Let it stand about 5 minutes so the fat can rise to the surface. Skim with a large spoon. You can also lightly pull a sheet of clean paper towel over the surface, letting the grease be absorbed. To degrease canned broth, refrigerate the unopened can. Simply spoon the congealed fat off the surface after opening the can.

Cutting Your Vegetables
Vegetables often take longer to cook than meats. Cut vegetables into small, thin pieces and place them on the bottom or near the sides of the slow cooker. Pay careful attention to the recipe instructions in order to cut vegetables to the proper size.

Foil to the Rescue
To easily lift a dish or a meat loaf out of the slow cooker, make foil handles according to the following directions.

• Tear off three 18×3-inch strips of heavy-duty foil. Crisscross the strips so they resemble the spokes of a wheel. Place your dish or food in the center of the strips.

• Pull the foil strips up and place into the slow cooker. Leave them in while you cook so you can easily lift the item out again when ready.

Food Safety Tips
If you do any advance preparation, such as trimming meat or cutting vegetables, make sure you keep the food covered and refrigerated until you're ready to start cooking. Store uncooked meats and vegetables separately. If you are preparing meat, poultry or fish, remember to wash your cutting board, utensils and hands before touching other foods.

Once your dish is cooked, don't keep it in the slow cooker too long. Foods need to be kept cooler than 40°F or hotter than 140°F to avoid the growth of harmful bacteria. Remove food to a clean container and cover and refrigerate as soon as possible. Do not reheat leftovers in the slow cooker. Use a microwave oven, the range-top or the oven for reheating.

Getting Ready

• Stir-frying can be broken down into two separate steps: (1) preparation of ingredients and (2) cooking. Because stir-frying requires constant attention during a relatively short cooking time, all ingredients should be cleaned, cut up, measured and arranged for easy access before you begin cooking.

• To guarantee that meats and vegetables cook evenly, cut them into equal-sized pieces according to the recipe directions. Also, it may be easier to slice meat and poultry that have been partially frozen first.

• Heavy-duty resealable plastic food storage bags are perfect for marinating ingredients. Any foods marinated longer than 20 minutes should be marinated in the refrigerator. Make sure to stir any mixtures containing cornstarch immediately before using to prevent lumping.

Cook It Up

• The kind of oil used for stir-frying is very important. Use vegetable oils such as peanut, corn, canola, soybean or a combination of these oils because they withstand high heat without smoking. Sesame oil, olive oil and butter burn easily.

• When the ingredients are ready to go and you're set to cook, heat the wok until it's very hot. Next, add the oil; it takes only about 30 seconds to heat thoroughly when added to a hot pan. Usually, the meat, poultry or seafood is stir-fried first and removed from the wok. Then the vegetables are added to the wok, followed by the sauce. Finally, the meat is returned to the wok to finish cooking or just heat through.

• You can successfully stir-fry a little food in a large wok (or skillet) but a lot of food in a little wok will bring disappointing results.

How Much of This=That?

If you don't have:	Use:
1 cup buttermilk	1 tablespoon lemon juice or vinegar plus milk to equal 1 cup (stir; let stand 5 minutes)
1 tablespoon cornstarch	2 tablespoons all-purpose flour or 2 teaspoons arrowroot.
1 cup beef or chicken broth	1 bouillon cube or 1 teaspoon granules mixed with 1 cup boiling water
1 small clove garlic	⅛ teaspoon garlic powder
1 tablespoon prepared mustard	1 teaspoon dry mustard
1 cup tomato sauce	½ cup tomato paste plus ½ cup cold water
1 teaspoon vinegar	2 teaspoons lemon juice
1 cup whole milk	1 cup skim milk plus 2 tablespoons melted butter
1 cup sour cream	1 cup plain yogurt

Common Weights and Measures

Dash = less than ⅛ teaspoon

½ tablespoon = 1½ teaspoons

1 tablespoon = 3 teaspoons

2 tablespoons = ⅛ cup

¼ cup = 4 tablespoons

⅓ cup = 5 tablespoons plus 1 teaspoon

½ cup = 8 tablespoons

¾ cup = 12 tablespoons

1 cup = 16 tablespoons

½ pint = 1 cup or 8 fluid ounces

1 pint = 2 cups or 16 fluid ounces

1 quart = 4 cups or 2 pints or 32 fluid ounces

1 gallon = 16 cups or 4 quarts

1 pound = 16 ounces

Is It Done Yet?

Use the following guides to test for doneness.

CASSEROLES
    until hot and bubbly
    until heated through
    until cheese melts

MEAT

Beef
    medium   140°F to 145°F
    well done 160°F

Veal
    medium   145°F to 150°F
    well done 160°F

Lamb
    medium   145°F
    well done 160°F

Pork
    well done 165°F to 170°F

POULTRY

Chicken
    until temperature in thigh
      is 180°F (whole bird)
    until chicken is no longer
      pink in center
    until temperature in breast
      is 170°F

SEAFOOD

Fish
    until fish begins to flake
      against the grain when
      tested with fork

Shrimp
    until shrimp are pink and
      opaque

SAUCES
    until (slightly) thickened

SOUPS
    until heated through

STEWS
    until meat is tender
    until vegetables are tender

VEGETABLES
    until crisp-tender
    until tender
    until browned

Metric Conversion Chart

VOLUME MEASUREMENTS (dry)

$\frac{1}{8}$ teaspoon = 0.5 mL
$\frac{1}{4}$ teaspoon = 1 mL
$\frac{1}{2}$ teaspoon = 2 mL
$\frac{3}{4}$ teaspoon = 4 mL
1 teaspoon = 5 mL
1 tablespoon = 15 mL
2 tablespoons = 30 mL
$\frac{1}{4}$ cup = 60 mL
$\frac{1}{3}$ cup = 75 mL
$\frac{1}{2}$ cup = 125 mL
$\frac{2}{3}$ cup = 150 mL
$\frac{3}{4}$ cup = 175 mL
1 cup = 250 mL
2 cups = 1 pint = 500 mL
3 cups = 750 mL
4 cups = 1 quart = 1 L

VOLUME MEASUREMENTS (fluid)

1 fluid ounce (2 tablespoons) = 30 mL
4 fluid ounces ($\frac{1}{2}$ cup) = 125 mL
8 fluid ounces (1 cup) = 250 mL
12 fluid ounces (1$\frac{1}{2}$ cups) = 375 mL
16 fluid ounces (2 cups) = 500 mL

WEIGHTS (mass)

$\frac{1}{2}$ ounce = 15 g
1 ounce = 30 g
3 ounces = 90 g
4 ounces = 120 g
8 ounces = 225 g
10 ounces = 285 g
12 ounces = 360 g
16 ounces = 1 pound = 450 g

DIMENSIONS

$\frac{1}{16}$ inch = 2 mm
$\frac{1}{8}$ inch = 3 mm
$\frac{1}{4}$ inch = 6 mm
$\frac{1}{2}$ inch = 1.5 cm
$\frac{3}{4}$ inch = 2 cm
1 inch = 2.5 cm

OVEN TEMPERATURES

250°F = 120°C
275°F = 140°C
300°F = 150°C
325°F = 160°C
350°F = 180°C
375°F = 190°C
400°F = 200°C
425°F = 220°C
450°F = 230°C

BAKING PAN SIZES

Utensil	Size in Inches/Quarts	Metric Volume	Size in Centimeters
Baking or Cake Pan (square or rectangular)	8×8×2	2 L	20×20×5
	9×9×2	2.5 L	23×23×5
	12×8×2	3 L	30×20×5
	13×9×2	3.5 L	33×23×5
Loaf Pan	8×4×3	1.5 L	20×10×7
	9×5×3	2 L	23×13×7
Round Layer Cake Pan	8×1½	1.2 L	20×4
	9×1½	1.5 L	23×4
Pie Plate	8×1¼	750 mL	20×3
	9×1¼	1 L	23×3
Baking Dish or Casserole	1 quart	1 L	—
	1½ quart	1.5 L	—
	2 quart	2 L	—

Acknowledgments

The publisher would like to thank the companies and organizations listed below for the use of their recipes and photographs in this publication.

Birds Eye®

Filippo Berio Olive Oil

GREY POUPON® Mustard

Hormel Foods Corporation

Hunt-Wesson, Inc.

Kikkoman International Inc.

Lee Kum Kee (USA) Inc.

Lipton®

National Honey Board

National Pork Producers Council

National Turkey Federation

Nestlé USA, Inc.

North Dakota Beef Commission

Perdue Farms Incorporated

Plochman, Inc.

The Procter & Gamble Company

Sunkist Growers

Index

Index

Index

Index